7 steps to freedom: how to overcome social anxiety

Julius Berger

Book description

In this book, you will learn how social anxiety develops, why it holds you back in many situations, and most importantly, how you can leave it behind, step by step. You will learn proven methods from the field of psychology, from cognitive behavioral therapy to mindfulness exercises and practical exposure techniques. With concrete examples, exercises, and helpful tips, the book shows you how to communicate more confidently, overcome inner blocks, and build a stable network. The focus is not only on reducing anxiety, but also on your personal development so that you can live a more open and fulfilling life.

About the author

Julius Berger is a person with a deep passion for charity and compassion. He enjoys helping others, listening to them and always having an open ear for their concerns and problems. He always gives his best with his tireless willingness to give advice and support. He walks through life with determination and assertiveness, working tirelessly to do what is best for others, even when that often means trying to please everyone.

Through his professional and volunteer work in the emergency services, he understands the perspective of both the affected and the professional. He distills his knowledge into easy-to-understand texts without sacrificing depth.

7 steps to freedom: how to overcome social anxiety

A practical book for bold everyday life, courageous encounters and new opportunities

Julius Berger

Do you like the book? Please rate it on Amazon, it would be a great help to me! Thank you very much.

If you have any questions or concerns, you can reach me at any time at: impressum.berger@proton.me.

Imprint
2. Edition, 2025
© 2025 Julius Berger – all rights reserved.

Address
Julius Berger
c/o Block Services
Stuttgarter Str. 106
70736 Fellbach
Deutschland/Germany

E-mail-contact
impressum.berger@proton.me

Inhaltsverzeichnis

Chapter 1: Introduction   4
Why this book?   5
What is social anxiety?   8
How you can use this book   11

Chapter 2: The roots of social anxiety   16
Biological and evolutionary foundations   17
Family influences and upbringing   20
Parenting styles and their influence   21
Social and cultural factors   25
Personal experiences and traumas   29

Chapter 3: Recognizing social anxiety   35
Typical symptoms   36
Differentiation from shyness   40
Core characteristics of social anxiety   41
Examples of shyness vs. social anxiety   42
How fear affects your everyday life   44
Professional challenges   44
Interpersonal relationships   45
Leisure and everyday life   46
Self-test: Where are you right now?   48
Summary and outlook   51

Chapter 4: The power of thoughts and feelings — 53
The cycle of negative thoughts — 54
Understanding negative automatic thoughts — 54
First exercises: Observe and reinterpret thoughts — 56
Perfectionism and exaggerated expectations — 58
Steps towards realistic self-assessment — 59
Self-esteem and self-acceptance — 61
When fear turns into self-criticism — 64
Self-compassion instead of self-accusation — 65

Chapter 5: Strategies against social anxiety — 69
Cognitive behavioral therapy (CBT) and its principles — 70
Facing fear step by step — 72
Structure of an exposure plan — 73
Mindfulness: consciously perceiving the moment — 75
Basic techniques of mindfulness — 76
Meditation: finding peace within — 79
How to establish a meditation practice — 81
Meditation in acute situations — 82
Other stress management methods — 83
Practical tips for implementation in everyday life — 85
Long-term effects and prospects — 87
Frequently asked questions — 89
Final thoughts: Your path is unique — 91

Chapter 6: Self-care and self-confidence — 93
Discover resources — 94
Establish positive beliefs — 98
The power of our convictions — 98
Detect and transform negative beliefs — 98
Anchoring positive beliefs in everyday life — 99
Typical hurdles when practicing new beliefs — 100
Dealing with setbacks — 102
Typical forms of setbacks — 102
Strategies for overcoming setbacks — 103

Building resilience - the art of coming back strong — 104
Stick with it in the long term and consolidate successes — 105
Conclusion: A stable path to self-care — 108

Chapter 7: Communication and social skills — 110
The basics of successful communication — 111
Active listening — 111
Self-revelation and authenticity — 112
Conflict resolution: arguing constructively and setting boundaries — 114
Master Networking — 118
Master small talk — 121
Summary and outlook — 124

Chapter 8: Finding support — 126
Involve friends, family and your social environment — 127
Professional help: therapy and counseling — 130
Online and self-help groups — 133
The path to a greater sense of community — 135
Summary and outlook — 137

Chapter 9: Looking ahead — 139
Visions for your future — 140
Finding meaning and personal development — 142
Discover new opportunities — 144
Gratitude and mindfulness in everyday life — 146
Summary: Life beyond fear — 148

Chapter 10: Conclusion and outlook — 151
Summary of the most important findings — 152
What happens next: your next steps — 154
Tools and outlook — 156
Concluding words — 157

Chapter 1: Introduction

Welcome to this book, which is designed to help you better understand social anxiety and how to deal with it constructively. Before we get into the details, however, it is important to set the stage: why this book, what exactly is social anxiety, and how can you best use what you read? Many people often consider self-help books to be pure theory or platitudes. This book, on the other hand, aims to provide you with a pragmatic, sound, and empathetic guide to help you on your personal journey.

Social anxiety is a problem that affects far more people than you might think. Too often, it is hidden behind the label „shyness" or phrases like „he or she is just an introvert". But social anxiety can severely limit your life: whether at work, with your family, with friends, or even when shopping at the supermarket, anyone who constantly fears being judged or devalued by others experiences stress and insecurity. This constant feeling can be very distressing, making life a constant balancing act between withdrawal and inner struggle.

The first chapter is an overview: It explains why this book was written and what you, the reader, can expect from it. Then we clarify what social anxiety actually is and how it manifests itself in everyday life - and how it differs from ordinary shyness or insecurity. Finally, we look at how you can use the following chapters to your advantage. After all, it's not just about accumulating knowledge, it's also about integrating it into your daily life in a very concrete way.

Why this book?

The idea for this book came from the recurring impression that many people who suffer from social anxiety often feel that they are alone. Although we live in a time of increased awareness of mental health and a proliferation of self-help resources, there is still uncertainty about taking one's anxiety seriously. Some people are not even aware that anxiety is an accepted and well-researched phenomenon in psychology and psychotherapy. Others notice that they are „somehow" anxious in social situations, but don't know where to turn or how to deal with it constructively.

A central goal of this book is to show you that you are not alone. More importantly, there are effective strategies that can help. Social anxiety is not a rigid life sentence that you must carry around with you forever. You can learn to understand your individual fear mechanisms, recognize their causes, and gradually find a new, more confident way of dealing with them.

The book offers a holistic approach. On the one hand, it draws on insights from psychology, particularly from areas such as cognitive behavioral therapy (CBT). Over the past few decades, this field has produced well-researched and proven methods for addressing anxiety in general and social anxiety in particular. On the other hand, the book is also shaped by practical experience and exchange with those affected. Theoretical knowledge is often dry and abstract without practice - the goal here is to provide examples that are understandable and hopefully motivate people to try new behaviors.

Another reason for writing this book is the increasing complexity of society. We live in an age that confronts us with social media, constant (self-)presentation, high external expectations, and a never-ending flood of information. At work, we are under pressure to perform, and in our relationships, we want to be harmonious and understanding while appearing assertive and confident. In all of these roles, social anxiety can have a particularly negative impact: The feeling of being judged or not being good enough is fueled by constant comparisons and high external demands.

This book does not want to stop at an isolated view („social anxiety as a pure clinical picture"), but rather places the topic in our modern context: What is the role of media influences, what is the role of our working world, and how does social anxiety affect interpersonal, often digitally mediated communication? Once we understand that social anxiety can also be fueled by social structures and cultural practices, it is often easier not to see ourselves as „defective" but to place our own feelings in a larger context.

At the same time, the goal of the book is to be as accessible as possible. Psychological terms are used to accurately reflect the concepts. Wherever possible, however, they are explained or illustrated with examples from everyday life. In addition, the writing style should be inviting, as if you were communicating with a person who, despite his expertise, is at eye level.

As the author of this book, it is especially important to me that you feel encouraged to take your experiences seriously and go one step further. Many people who suffer from social anxiety have come to terms with their fears in some way. They may have developed a lifestyle that avoids the triggering factors as much as possible. However, avoidance is rarely a satisfactory long-term solution because it means missing out on potentially valuable experiences and relationships. The message of this book is: It is possible to take the first step. The approaches and exercises presented here will not eliminate all anxiety from the world overnight-that would be unrealistic. But they can set in motion a process that brings us closer to a life in which we can act more freely.

At the same time, it should not be hidden that there are situations in which professional help is essential. This book cannot and is not intended to be a substitute for psychotherapy. If your social anxieties are extremely distressing to you and are blocking you in many areas of your life, it makes sense to consider therapeutic support. However, this advice is not meant to scare you, but to encourage you: the methods of behavior therapy and other therapeutic schools are not only for extreme cases. They can also help people who „only" experience stage fright or severe insecurity in certain situations.

Some readers may wonder if they are really affected or just a bit introverted. There is no general answer to this question because social anxiety has many facets. You may be just starting out, feeling a vague sense of insecurity, and just want a few tips to help you feel more confident. Or maybe your anxiety has deeper roots and you want to try more advanced methods. Wherever you are, the chapters of this book are structured so that you can pick and choose the knowledge and exercises that are right for you.

In summary, this book has been written to be a reliable companion on your journey out of social anxiety. It aims to provide space for reflection, to impart sound knowledge, and to encourage you to take practical steps. You will find theoretical foundations as well as concrete exercises and suggestions for your everyday life.

What is social anxiety?

Before we get into techniques, exercises, and more in-depth analysis, it is important to understand exactly what we are talking about. „Social anxiety is a well-defined term in psychology: it is a form of anxiety disorder in which people fear being judged negatively in social or performance situations. This fear of possible criticism, embarrassment, or rejection is so strong that it causes stress and sometimes even physical symptoms.

But what distinguishes social anxiety from general shyness or nervousness? Almost everyone knows the feeling of blushing or sweaty hands before a presentation. This is completely normal and even biologically beneficial: our bodies activate the sympathetic nervous system to be alert and responsive when we are in a challenging situation. In the case of social anxiety, however, this feeling occurs not only in such „exceptional situations," but can also occur in everyday social interactions - for example, when meeting colleagues during your lunch break or having to show your ticket on the bus.

An important factor is the intensity and duration of the anxiety: people who suffer from social anxiety don't just experience a brief butterflies in their stomach or a nervous sweat. Often, just thinking about an upcoming situation - such as a party or meeting - is associated with prolonged worry. You imagine all the things that could go wrong („What if I say the wrong thing and everyone laughs?"), doubt your own abilities („I'm not interesting enough to hold a conversation anyway"), and sometimes this leads to real avoidance strategies: canceling invitations, missing important professional appointments, or leaving situations as early as possible.

Social anxiety can also be limited to specific areas. Some people are particularly afraid of public speaking or being the center of attention. They get nervous when they have to give a presentation or say a few words at a party. Others have more difficulty with interpersonal interactions, such as making small talk in large groups or meeting new people. In all cases, however, the fear of negative evaluation is central, and this concern is disproportionate to the actual situation.

In professional jargon, the term „social phobia" is often used. The term phobia describes a strong fear that goes beyond mere caution or flight instinct. It is often irrational, persisting even when the mind knows that the fear is exaggerated or unlikely. Many people try to hide their fears because they are ashamed of being „irrational. But therein lies the dilemma: even when your mind tells you that there is no real threat, the feeling of fear is often stronger than logic.

In addition, social anxiety often affects self-esteem. If you are constantly worried about what others think of you, if you fear that you are not good enough, this has a negative impact on your self-image. It can lead to brooding after a conversation („Why did I tell that joke? It was totally stupid"), self-blame („I'm so boring, why would anyone want to spend time with me?"), or seemingly innocuous statements that turn into negative beliefs („I'm just not cut out for groups").

Social anxiety may worsen over time. You have repeatedly experienced being very nervous and uncomfortable in a social context. This reinforces the expectation that the next similar situation will be uncomfortable. The sense of control disappears and the person feels increasingly at the mercy of others. Through avoidance, they try to escape the seemingly simplest dangers - but this leads to a diminishing chance of having a positive or at least neutral experience in such situations.

Studies show that social anxiety is relatively common. It is one of the most common anxiety disorders worldwide, along with other forms such as agoraphobia (fear of open spaces or crowds) or generalized anxiety disorder (constant worrying). The number of unreported cases may be even higher, as not all people who experience social anxiety receive a diagnosis or seek professional help.

It is important to note that social anxiety can occur in a variety of contexts and is not limited to the classic example of „speaking in front of an audience". Social media can also be the site of social anxiety: Fear of derogatory comments, not getting enough likes, or making a fool of yourself in public can be a major stress factor. Many people who tend to be shy in real life sometimes take to the Internet - but at the same time, the digital world can also trigger new fears, such as the fear of hate comments or the compulsion to constantly present oneself.

In summary, social anxiety is a complex issue. At its core is a deep-seated fear of being perceived negatively or rejected by others. This book will help you understand this core: how it arises, why it persists, and how to challenge it. On the other hand, it gives you tools to help you reduce this fear step by step and to help you gain new experiences. The fact that you are holding this book in your hands already shows that you have taken the first step: you want to make a change. We will build on that in the chapters that follow.

How you can use this book

A book is only as good as its application. Theoretical knowledge is important, but it is in practice that it unfolds its full power. Therefore, this subchapter is intended to give you a guide on how to work with the book - so that it does not remain a mere reading, but becomes an active companion on your journey.

Go through chapter by chapter

Of course, you can also read the book in a linear fashion, starting with Chapter 1 and systematically working your way through to the end. This has the advantage that you benefit from a logical progression: first you understand the basics (what is social anxiety, where does it come from?), then you learn to recognize your own symptoms and mechanisms, and finally you learn how to put what you have learned into practice. The chapters often build on each other, so that you gradually gain a deeper understanding.

Targeted lookup

Sometimes, however, you may have an urgent need, such as finding out how to deal with a specific situation in your daily life. In this case, you can easily jump directly to the chapter that will help you the most (e.g., the chapter on exposure techniques or the chapter on communication skills). In this case, the book is organized to make it relatively easy to find the key topics. However, it is a good idea to read the previous chapters as soon as possible to put everything into context.

Reflect and take notes

As you read, you will come across numerous exercises, reflection questions and examples that address you directly or encourage you to reflect. Take notes: What does the exercise trigger in you? What do you understand immediately, what remains unclear, where do your biggest "aha" moments lie? It's best to create a separate notebook or digital document in which you record your thoughts. This way, a personal space for reflection grows alongside the reading material, which you can later add to or rearrange as needed.

Taking practical exercises seriously

Throughout this book you will find practical exercises-breathing techniques, mindfulness exercises, small behavioral experiments, or simple homework assignments. These exercises are at the heart of your development, because only by trying new behaviors will your experience begin to change. Even if an exercise seems trivial at first („Why should I watch my breath now?"), it's worth doing. Sometimes it is the seemingly simple methods that are surprisingly effective, because they change the way you look at your fears or show you that you are in control even in seemingly hopeless moments.

Don't shy away from small steps

Many people with social anxiety want to see quick results. This is understandable: anyone who has suffered for a long time wants to feel relief right away. And yes, if you really commit to the exercises, you will see some progress soon. However, it is wise not to be too perfectionistic. Change is a process that takes time. There will be setbacks, that's normal. The important thing is to keep going and to appreciate small successes. Even expressing your needs in a group for the first time or making eye contact in a conversation can be a big step forward.

Stay continuous

A book can inspire, motivate, and encourage. But you have to stick with it. Reading it once and then forgetting it won't have the desired effect. It's a matter of gradually integrating the content into your daily life. That's why it's a good idea to set aside specific times to work on the book and your notes. Some people like to read and think for 15 to 20 minutes every day. Others set aside one weekend a month. Find your own rhythm.

Search professional help

Although this book is designed as a self-help book, it can be very helpful to start or continue therapy at the same time. Many therapists appreciate it when their clients independently engage with literature on the subject, as this complements the therapeutic work. If you are already in therapy, you can discuss individual exercises or passages from this book with your therapist. This sometimes opens doors to deeper insights.

Exchange with others

The issues of shyness and anxiety often isolate us - we feel we are alone with them. The book recommends that you talk to others whenever possible. This can be people you trust in your personal environment or support groups (online or offline) where people with similar difficulties are active. It often helps to see that you are not alone. You can also share experiences, tips, and encouragement.

Compassion for yourself

The most important thing is to be patient and kind to yourself. There will be times when you don't want to do an exercise because it scares you or you have doubts. You may put the book down for a while because your life is stressful right now. That's okay. Try not to beat yourself up for taking these breaks. Overcoming social anxiety is a process of many small steps, and each step will get you further. Treating yourself with kindness and having a healthy understanding of the challenges you face are often the best ingredients for lasting change.

Finding your own way

With all the advice and techniques you will find in this book, it is important that you find your own way. People are different, and not every method will work for every personality or life situation. You may find that meditation is very appealing to you, while a certain type of exposure training doesn't work for you-or vice versa. That's perfectly normal. Try it out and be open to new experiences. At the same time, of course, you can omit or adapt methods you don't like at all. The book gives you a wide range to choose from.

Think of this book as a toolbox that provides you with different tools to help you better manage your social anxiety. You decide which tools to use and when to use them. The most important thing is to stay on the ball and keep asking yourself, „How am I doing with this right now? What would help me now? What can I plan for tomorrow?

If you approach the subject with an open, curious mind and allow yourself to make mistakes and grow, you will get a lot out of this book. Of course, we will return to these points again and again as we move through the chapters. You should know that the learning process is never linear. There will be times when you feel great and notice that your fears are diminishing, but there will also be times when doubts or old patterns come back to haunt you. This is all part of real change.

The first chapter has shown you why this book exists, what social anxiety is, and how you can put the content to practical use. This will give you a solid foundation from which to delve, step by step, into the following chapters. There, you will learn more about the causes and mechanisms of social anxiety, learn strategies to gently counteract it, and develop a personalized plan to help you live a more empowered and anxiety-free life.

If you are already feeling a tingling sensation or are curious about what will happen next, then you are in the right place. Let your curiosity and motivation guide you, even if they are still quiet. The very willingness to engage with your inner self is a powerful signal. The next chapter is about the roots of social anxiety: we will look at the biological, family, and social aspects that explain why you may feel the way you do. This understanding is the foundation for everything else.

This concludes the first chapter. You now have a rough idea of how the book is organized and what it is about. Grab a pen or open a document on your computer and write down what concerns you most when you think about social situations. You may also want to define your goal: „Where do I want to be at the end of this book? Use this goal as a guide-and if, as you read, you find that the goal changes or becomes more specific, that's also a good sign that you're actively working on it.

Remember, you are going at your own pace. And every small step is a success.

Chapter 2: The roots of social anxiety

Social anxiety does not just „drop out of the sky" or result from a single experience that made you feel very insecure. Rather, it is the result of a complex interplay of biological, familial, social, and individual factors. Understanding how these influences have developed over the course of your life can help us understand the mechanisms behind anxiety. This deeper understanding is not only interesting, but also very helpful in realizing that your social anxiety is neither a „character flaw" nor a purely arbitrary whim of your psyche. It has a history and follows certain patterns that have developed over time. In this chapter, we will explore why some people experience social anxiety more than others. We will focus on four areas: biological and evolutionary foundations, family influences and upbringing, social and cultural factors, and personal experiences and traumas.

Biological and evolutionary foundations

To understand why we humans experience social anxiety, it is worth taking a look at our biological and evolutionary past. At first glance, it seems paradoxical that we can be anxious about meeting other people, even though we are social creatures by nature. However, this paradox reveals a millennia-old evolutionary history in which social interaction was essential for survival, but could also pose real dangers.

The need for social bonding
Of all mammals, humans are arguably the most dependent on social bonds and care from birth. A human baby cannot feed itself or protect itself from danger. It needs the immediate closeness and attention of its caregivers to survive. This need for attachment continues throughout our lives, albeit in different forms. Even as adults, we feel safer and more secure when we are part of a group or community that supports us emotionally and, ideally, practically.

From an evolutionary psychology perspective, living in a group was essential for survival in a hostile environment. Those who were isolated were at greater risk of falling prey to predators or hostile tribes. At the same time, cooperation was a success factor: only those who worked well as a team could hunt together, share food, and warn each other of danger. This interplay between bonding and group living is deeply rooted in our genetic makeup and continues to underlie our social behavior today.

The flip side: rejection and exclusion
Surrounding yourself with people allows you to enjoy closeness, protection, and fellowship. But being social also means exposing yourself to the judgment of others. In the small tribal communities of thousands of years ago, being ostracized from the group could be life-threatening. Ostracism meant not only the loss

of social recognition, but often the loss of food, shelter, or help with illness and injury.

Over the course of evolution, a highly sensitive alarm and warning system evolved: any sign of rejection or negative evaluation could threaten survival. This explains why we are still so sensitive to criticism, ridicule, or rejection. Even though there is little physical danger in being excluded from a group in modern society, our bodies still take such threats very seriously. This explains why social anxiety (or fear of embarrassment) can lead to severe physical reactions: a racing heart, sweaty hands, and an increase in the stress hormone cortisol are typical signs that our bodies are preparing for a „fight or flight" situation.

Genetic factors

Although we all carry a certain amount of fear of rejection, the intensity varies from person to person. Some of these differences may be due to genetic influences. Twin studies have shown that anxiety disorders, including social anxiety, are inherited to some degree. There is no single „anxiety mutation," but many gene variants work together to influence our neurobiology.

A key area in the brain is the amygdala, which is responsible for the emotional processing of fear and threat. In people with high levels of social anxiety, the amygdala may be particularly sensitive and react more quickly to potential danger. The neurotransmitters serotonin, dopamine, and norepinephrine also play a role. Certain gene variants, for example, can cause someone to react more strongly to stress hormones or to recover less well from negative experiences. These physiological predispositions do not mean that social anxiety is inevitable, but they can increase the risk.

Temperament and personality traits

In addition to genetic factors, there are also temperamental traits that can influence the risk of developing social anxiety and become apparent in early childhood. One of the most commonly studied traits is the Behavioral Inhibition System (BIS). Children with a strong BIS are very sensitive to new stimuli or unfamiliar people and situations. They are more cautious, anxious and tend to withdraw rather than approach strangers with curiosity.

This inhibited temperament can develop into social anxiety later in life, but it doesn't have to. Much depends on the environment in which a child grows up, how their parents deal with them, and whether they have positive experiences with their peers. However, it has been shown that some people are more prone to anxiety from birth, while others tend to be more curious and outgoing throughout their lives.

The role of neuroplasticity

Fortunately, our biology is not an immutable fate. The brain is plastic, meaning that it can change and adapt well into old age. This explains why cognitive behavioral therapy (CBT), exposure training, and other psychological approaches can actually leave biological traces: When you learn to expose yourself to new social situations in a controlled way and have positive experiences, new neural connections are formed. The amygdala can learn to respond less intensely to perceived threats, while areas in the prefrontal cortex that allow for more rational control of anxiety are strengthened.

The message is encouraging: even if you have a higher biological or genetic susceptibility to social anxiety, you are not doomed to suffer from it for life. You can „reprogram" your brain through training, therapy, and self-help strategies. However, this process requires patience and persistence-qualities that we will emphasize throughout this book.

Conclusion on the biological-evolutionary roots

All in all, a look at our biological and evolutionary past shows that social anxieties have understandable roots. We are social creatures for whom acceptance was once essential for survival and still plays an important role today. Our brains are wired to approach sensitive social situations with caution. In addition, there are genetic and temperamental influences that can increase or decrease the risk of social anxiety. Despite this predisposition, there is much you can do. New learning experiences can gradually break old cycles of fear. This chapter was important to show you that you are neither „strange" nor „completely helpless"-there is a rational explanation for everything, and there are ways to counteract these mechanisms with knowledge and training.

Family influences and upbringing

Having dealt with the biological foundations, we now turn to the next level: the family and social environment in which we grow up. Our very first experiences are usually with our family, be it our parents, grandparents, or other caregivers. This is where we learn not only how to behave in social situations, but also how to deal with fears and insecurities.

Attachment theory and early relationships

British psychiatrist John Bowlby's attachment theory is a powerful reminder of how formative our early relationship experiences are. A child who develops a secure attachment to his or her caregivers experiences the world as a place that, for all its unpredictability, is fundamentally safe and predictable. The child develops a positive „internal working model" of self and others: „I am valuable and others will help me when I am in need.

Conversely, an insecure or even disorganized attachment can develop when caregivers' reactions are not very predictable or when they are emotionally or physically unavailable. The child then learns that the world is full of threats and that it can be left alone. Later, this may manifest as increased social anxiety due to a lack of confidence that one is in good hands in social situations. While this is not a deterministic path (not every insecurely attached child will develop social anxiety disorder), the risk is significantly increased.

Parenting styles and their influence

Parents and other caregivers consciously or unconsciously exhibit certain parenting styles. These have a major impact on our personality and self-esteem. Simply put, there are three main categories: authoritarian, permissive, and authoritative parenting styles.

Authoritarian parenting style: This style is characterized by strict rules and high expectations. Children who grow up in an authoritarian household often have little room to make their own decisions. Instead, they learn to follow rules and prohibitions and face harsh punishment or emotional distance if they break the rules. If a child is constantly having to conform and is afraid of criticism or rejection, this can be a breeding ground for social anxiety. The message is: „Watch what you say and do, or you'll be rejected or punished. The child internalizes this threatening climate and later transfers it to other social contexts.

Permissive parenting style: Here, parents are very lenient, setting few rules and rarely taking action. These children usually have a lot of freedom, but often don't know what their limits are. A lack of guidance and clear structures can foster independence, but it can also foster anxiety because the child lacks cues and support. This can lead to insecurity in social situations where it is not clear how to assert oneself or set limits in relation to others.

Authoritative parenting style: This style is considered a healthy middle ground. On the one hand, children are given rules and guidance, and on the other hand, they are given space to make their own decisions and opinions. They learn that they are valuable even when they make mistakes or disagree. This promotes a positive self-image and reduces the likelihood of extreme anxiety in social contexts.

These categories are idealized, of course. In reality, there is often a mix of different elements, and cultural backgrounds can also shape parenting styles. However, it is important to recognize that a child who is either over- or under-controlled is more likely to enter adulthood with anxiety.

Family beliefs and communication patterns

The family is not only a place of education, but also a cosmos of beliefs, rituals, and ways of thinking. This is where you automatically learn what is „normal" and what is not. For example, if your parents constantly talk about how important it is what others think of you, this belief can become deeply rooted in your consciousness. Or if your family often says things like „Don't stand out" or „Don't show any weakness," then you learn that social interactions are risky and you'd better not give anyone anything to criticize.

How you deal with your feelings can also influence later social anxiety. In some families, feelings are discussed openly, and there is room for anger, sadness, and joy without judgment. In other families, anything that might seem „weak" or „embarrassing" is swept under the rug. If you didn't learn as a child that it's okay to be scared and to talk about it, you may develop inhibitions about trusting others later in life. This can exacerbate social anxiety because you always feel like you have to put on an act.

An example of this is perfectionism. If parents constantly demand perfection and criticize every mistake the child makes, it can lead to a strong pressure to perform. Anyone who grows up in such an environment quickly ties their self-esteem to flawless performance - mistakes are a no-go. But perfection is impossible, especially in unpredictable social interactions. As a result, you are constantly afraid of saying the wrong thing or making a negative impression, which can increase stress in social situations.

Sibling dynamics and role assignments

In addition to parents, siblings are important socialization factors. Sibling relationships can be close and supportive, or they can be competitive and rivalrous. Sometimes one child in a family is assigned the role of „shy" or „sensitive," while another is seen as „daring. Such role attributions can unconsciously cause the child who is attributed with shyness to internalize this trait more and more. They then conform to family expectations and have difficulty trying new, more confident behaviors.

In addition, children are very observant of how their older siblings handle social situations. For example, if an older brother has major problems with bullying at school, the younger child may become more sensitive to such risks. They may become more withdrawn or learn to avoid certain situations in order to avoid „going through the same thing. Thus, family influence is a very complex web of direct and indirect messages that lay the foundation for our later social behavior.

Conclusion on the family environment

The family is the place where you learn basic beliefs about yourself and others. Negative or fearful attitudes can become entrenched here and contribute to pronounced social anxiety later in life. However, the family environment is only one of many factors. Some children from difficult families develop amazing self-confidence, while others from sheltered families are deeply insecure as adults. Genetics, temperament, and other life circumstances always play a role. However, it can be very helpful for you to think about what family rules, beliefs, and parenting styles you inherited from your childhood - and whether you are still using them unconsciously. Only when you are aware of this will you be able to consciously question and, if necessary, break old patterns.

Social and cultural factors

So far we have talked about the biological level and the family. But you do not grow up in a vacuum; you are part of a society that cultivates certain values, norms, and ideals. Culture and the zeitgeist also have a major influence on our social anxieties - often more than we realize. Whether you grow up in a big city or in the country, in a traditional society or in a postmodern, individualistic culture, all of this can shape the way you perceive and evaluate social situations.

Social roles and expectations

Every society has certain role expectations that determine how individuals should behave. For example, you may live in a society where it is considered rude to avoid eye contact or not answer questions clearly. In other societies, it may be frowned upon to speak too directly or to show your feelings openly. Failure to meet these expectations may result in subtle or overt negative reactions.

These social norms operate in the background, often without being explicitly written down, but they are powerful nonetheless. Sometimes you only learn about them when you violate them. As a child or adolescent, you may develop a sense of not belonging if you feel that you are different from the crowd. For some, this manifests itself in creeping social anxiety; for others, it manifests itself in rebellion. But rebellion can also trigger anxiety because it puts you on the social sidelines, where you experience the fear of rejection all over again.

Pressure to perform and a culture of comparison

In many modern societies, there is a lot of pressure to perform. We are expected to get good grades in school, succeed in college or vocational training, and then get a prestigious job. At the same time, we are expected to be socially competent, attractive, fit, and always „in a good mood. This quickly leads to a situation where we are constantly being compared: Who presents themselves best? Who has the most friends, the most followers, the most exciting hobbies?

Especially in the age of social media, this pressure to compare has increased exponentially. On platforms like Instagram or TikTok, people often present only the best sides of their lives - aesthetic vacation photos, smiling faces, and perfect outfits. This can create the impression that everyone else is living a flawless and exciting life, while you are ordinary, unremarkable, or even inferior. This phenomenon can fuel social anxiety as you feel the constant pressure to be perfect as well. Fear of virtual judgment - in the form of negative comments or lack of likes - can trigger real anxiety because our brains have limited ability to distinguish between digital and analog rejection.

Cultural differences in feelings of shame and guilt

Another cultural dimension is the way in which shame and guilt are dealt with. In some cultures, shame is a particularly strong emotion. Anyone who does not conform, who „embarrasses" the family, or who violates social norms, not only triggers a negative feeling in himself, but also has a direct impact on the reputation of the family or group. This creates additional pressure to avoid making mistakes in social situations. People from such cultures may be more likely to develop social anxiety because they perceive the risk of disappointing or embarrassing someone as particularly high.

In individualistic cultures, on the other hand, feelings of guilt about having done something wrong tend to be more of a problem. Here, social anxiety may arise from a desire to be seen as competent, independent, and successful. Showing weakness or needing help goes against the ideal of the „strong individual. The vicious cycle is obvious: because you're afraid to openly communicate your anxiety (because it might be seen as a weakness), it often intensifies.

Technological progress and urban lifestyle
We should also not forget that for many people, living in big cities or densely populated regions can mean an excess of social contact. In a subway full of people you meet every day, you're constantly being watched or judged in some way - at least you feel that way. The noise level, the hustle and bustle, the crowds: these are all stressors that can create a certain amount of tension, especially for people who are already sensitive to stimuli.

On top of this, technological advances are constantly enabling new forms of communication, such as videoconferencing or virtual team meetings, where you need to be in the picture at all times. Some people find this even more threatening because they are in a kind of self-observation (the famous camera image of themselves) and automatically pay attention to their own appearance. If you are already insecure, this constant situation of „being seen" can exacerbate your social anxiety.

The pressure of social success narratives
Our society often presents us with stories of successful social behavior. It starts with Hollywood movies: the main character handles difficult social situations with flying colors, wins the love of his or her life in the end, or receives sensational recognition. In casting shows or reality TV formats, we also see people who act with apparent confidence on camera and are rewarded for it. This

constant exposure to success stories can create a distorted image: „Everyone else can do it, so why do I have such a hard time?"

What is often missing is a realistic portrayal of insecurity and fear. This creates the impression that if you want to get anywhere in life, you have to be comfortable in the spotlight. If you don't make it, it's your own fault or you're just not talented. These social narratives create pressure. Individuals experience a discrepancy between their own experiences („I feel overwhelmed") and expectations („You have to be confident"). This discrepancy can fuel social anxiety massively.

Conclusion on social factors

Our culture, time, and social environment shape our understanding of normality and success. They also determine how we perceive and value anxiety, especially social anxiety. An achievement-oriented, self-expression-oriented environment can reinforce existing dispositions to social anxiety. However, this influence can also be used in a positive way: When we realize that many of our fears are rooted in social norms and expectations, we can begin to question them. We don't have to follow every trend or meet every expectation. Reflecting on our own position in relation to social demands and developing more self-determined values can be an important step in overcoming social anxiety.

Personal experiences and traumas

The most individual and often most painful level at which social anxiety arises is through personal experience, from bullying to traumatic events. Even if you are naturally robust and have had a stable family environment, stressful experiences at school, with friends, or at work can leave deep scars. Conversely, a security-oriented or sensitive personality combined with critical key experiences can lead to the intensification of social anxieties.

Bullying and exclusion

Bullying is one of the most common causes of social anxiety. Anyone who is systematically bullied - whether at school, in training, at work or on the Internet - suffers long-term negative social experiences. It often takes the form of humiliation, teasing, rumors, or targeted exclusion. Victims lose faith in the fairness of others and feel helpless. Even when the bullying stops, the emotional scars are often long-lasting: situations that remind the victim of past humiliations can trigger new fears and withdrawal.

A tragic aspect of bullying is that it is not uncommon for victims to blame themselves („I'm not good enough," „I'm ugly," „I'm uninteresting"). These internalized beliefs feed and perpetuate social anxiety because they create the expectation of being negatively judged or rejected in the future.

Embarrassing or traumatizing experiences

Perhaps you have had an embarrassing experience that you still remember years later. A failed presentation where you lost your train of thought while all eyes were on you, or a party where you stood in front of the others stuttering and blushing. Such experiences can become deeply embedded in our memory. Our brains tend to remember negative or particularly unpleasant experiences more vividly. Even though the objective significance of these situations may not have been great, the subjective perception can be extremely strong.

Traumatic experiences such as (sexual) abuse, physical violence, or other injuries are even more severe. Trauma can shatter a person's basic trust in others and leave them feeling fundamentally insecure. They may feel a pervasive sense of distrust in social situations because they have learned that other people can be dangerous to them. This can develop into acute social anxiety, in which even neutral interactions are perceived as potentially threatening.

Repetition patterns and generalization

What often happens with negative experiences is called generalization. For example, in 7th grade, you repeatedly experience derogatory comments from your classmates, perhaps because you dress differently or have interests that don't conform to the norm. Over time, you develop the belief: „If I'm with people my own age, I'm bound to be laughed at again." The specific attitude of „class 7, certain clique" quickly becomes a general pattern: „I can't assert myself in groups, everyone rejects me.

There may also be unconscious patterns of repetition: you find yourself repeatedly drawn to situations that reawaken the old trauma. This may sound contradictory at first, but in psychology this is called repetition compulsion: on an unconscious level we try to cope with the old experience in a new situation, but this often fails and the fear is perpetuated.

Key experiences, the positive turnaround

Fortunately, there are also positive key experiences. Many people report that a particular achievement - such as a successful speech, a constructive conversation, or unusually positive feedback - marked the turning point. Such „counterevidence" to one's negative self-image can be a powerful impetus to break out of the vicious cycle of social anxiety. The catch, however, is that it is often difficult to allow such experiences of success when one has been deeply hurt before. This is why we try to create such success experiences through exposure training or by finding new, safe social contexts in therapeutic work or in self-help strategies.

The inner self-talk

Personal experiences are not only stored in our memory, but also colored by the way we talk to ourselves about them. Our so-called „inner dialogues" are often automatic: „I made a fool of myself again. It was obvious, everything always goes wrong with me". Such automatic thoughts increase anxiety. On the other hand, if we learn to be more forgiving and constructive with ourselves, old wounds can heal. Failure in a social situation then becomes a learning experience rather than proof of one's inadequacy.

Conclusion on personal experiences and traumas

Social anxiety may be triggered by personal experiences. Negative or traumatic experiences leave a deep impression and can exacerbate an existing vulnerability (biological, familial, or social). Sometimes it is a single key moment, sometimes a chain of events that fuels our anxiety. However, these experiences are not set in stone: With targeted change work, such as psychotherapy, support groups, or individual exercises, these memories can be re-evaluated and the associated potential for anxiety reduced. It takes courage and determination to confront painful memories, but it's worth it because it helps you gradually regain control of your life.

Summary: A complex puzzle of causes

In this chapter we have seen how diverse the roots of social anxiety can be. They lie in our biology and evolution, which teaches us to seek social attachments while fearing rejection. They continue in our family environment, where we internalize certain parenting styles and beliefs. On a societal and cultural level, we encounter norms and expectations that further shape and sometimes pressure us. Finally, our very personal experiences-some positive, but many negative-come into play and can undermine our confidence in our social skills.

All of these factors do not operate in isolation, but influence each other. If you feel that several of these levels are intertwined in your life, this explains why your social anxieties can be so persistent. At the same time, this understanding offers many starting points: you may discover that certain cultural ideals are putting unnecessary pressure on you - then you can learn to question these ideals. Or you may realize that your family's communication was characterized by a fear of making mistakes-and you can consciously work to create a more open culture of error in your current life.

The following chapter is designed to help you better identify and classify your social anxieties. We will talk about typical symptoms, highlight the difference between shyness and social anxiety, and look at how anxiety can affect everyday life. There is also a self-test that will give you an initial indication of where you stand in relation to your social anxiety. This knowledge is important for defining your personal goals: Where do you want to go and what aspects of your fear do you want to address first?

Remember that it's normal to feel a little overwhelmed by the complexity of the causes. There are many puzzle pieces that fit together. But each piece that you recognize and contextualize is a step toward understanding-and understanding is the basis for change. You won't be able to „fix" everything right away, but you can start to break new ground. If reading this chapter has reminded you of certain situations from your childhood, adolescence, or recent past, take a moment to reflect on them or make notes.

You may also have had an „aha" experience about your family or cultural background. You may have become aware of patterns that you previously considered „normal" but that suddenly make sense in the context of social anxiety („No wonder I am so anxious when [...] happens all the time in my family"). Use these insights to be more kind to yourself. Understanding that there are reasons for your fears can be very relieving. It shows you that you are not just acting on a whim, but that your behavior is rooted in your past experiences and biology.

At the same time, it is important to realize that you are not „doomed" to stay this way forever. Our biology is adaptable, family influences can be questioned, social expectations can be critically reflected upon, and personal experiences can be seen in a new light. This process is not easy, but if you engage in it, you will find that step by step you gain more self-determination. Not only do you develop a new understanding of yourself, but you often develop more empathy for others who also struggle with anxiety.

In the next chapter, we'll take a closer look at the symptoms of social anxiety and how it can manifest itself in everyday life. Armed with this knowledge, you'll be well prepared to try various strategies and techniques to help you reduce your social anxiety. An important principle here is to give yourself the time you need. Change is a process, not a sprint. If you are ready to embark on this journey, you have already taken the most important step: you have decided to stop running from your fear and instead understand and face it.

Whatever your personal reasons, you don't have to be ashamed or justify yourself. Every story is unique, and everyone has the right to find their own way to deal with it. Rest assured that everything you learn in this chapter is not just a theoretical inventory, but something you can apply in your everyday life. When you realize that your fear is part of a larger story that you have helped to write (and are still helping to write), it becomes clear that you also have the chance to write another chapter in the future.

With this thought, we close Chapter Two. Take a few minutes to reflect before you continue reading. You have just received a lot of information - information that is important for laying the foundation for your self-work and possible therapeutic steps. Write down what impressed or touched you most, what questions remained unanswered, and what memories resurfaced. In the following chapters, you will have the opportunity to explore much of this in depth, to question it, and to address it with concrete tools.

Chapter 3: Recognizing social anxiety

In the previous chapters, we learned why this book was written, what social anxiety disorders are in general, and what causes them - from biological predisposition and family background to social influences and personal experiences. All of these factors form the background to a phenomenon that can manifest itself very differently from one person to the next: While one person may feel panic especially when giving a presentation, another may find it difficult to even start a conversation with strangers. Before we look at strategies and techniques for overcoming social anxiety in the following chapters, it is important to take a closer look at social anxiety: How do you recognize social anxiety in your life?

Therefore, this third chapter is entirely devoted to recognition. We look at typical symptoms, both physical and psychological. We also draw a clear line between shyness and true social anxiety - because not everything that feels like a little insecurity is a clinical phenomenon that needs treatment. We also look at how social anxiety can specifically affect everyday life: work, relationships, leisure - everything can be affected. Finally, you will find a self-test that will give you at least an initial assessment of where you currently stand. This is not intended as a clinical diagnosis, but rather as a guide to help you identify which aspects may be most relevant to you.

Make yourself comfortable and take your time with this chapter. The better you understand your own situation, the more effectively you can address the relevant issues later.

Typical symptoms

When people talk about „social anxiety," they often think of blushing in front of a group or feeling insecure in a conversation. But social anxiety is more than just butterflies. It often comes with a whole range of typical symptoms that affect both the body and the mind. In this section, we would like to describe these symptoms in more detail so that you can get an idea of whether and how they occur in your own everyday life.

Physical symptoms
Palpitations, tachycardia
One of the most common symptoms of social anxiety is palpitations. Often the heart seems to race, sometimes it even seems to jump out of the chest. This accelerated heartbeat is a natural response of the sympathetic nervous system that prepares the body for a perceived threat.

Sweating
Many people describe heavy sweating, especially on the hands, feet, or under the armpits. Sweaty, clammy hands are also possible. This symptom can make people feel even more self-conscious because it can be visible to others and cause even more embarrassment.

Shiver
Some people experience tremors in their fingers, knees, or even their whole body. This trembling is often the result of increased adrenaline levels. Similar to sweating, a vicious cycle can develop: the fear of trembling increases inner tension and intensifies the trembling.

Nausea and gastrointestinal complaints

We know "butterflies in the stomach" from positive excitement, but with social anxiety, it quickly turns into unpleasant pressure or a knot in the stomach. Some people then feel as if they are about to vomit, others suffer from diarrhea or constipation. The digestive system reacts very sensitively to anxiety and stress.

Breathing difficulties

Shortness of breath or a feeling of not getting enough air are other typical symptoms. Breathing may become shallow, causing the body to panic even more - signaling a lack of oxygen and increasing anxiety.

Muscle tension

Fear causes our bodies to contract. In the case of social anxiety, this can lead to generalized muscle tension, whether in the neck, shoulders, or back. Sometimes this can even lead to chronic pain or tension headaches over time.

The intensity of these physical symptoms can vary. Some people experience only a mild tingling sensation, while others are paralyzed by a racing heart or heavy sweating. It is important to remember that these symptoms are real physical reactions - not signs of weakness or imagination. They are a normal part of the human stress response, but in social anxiety they occur in situations that are not objectively life threatening.

Psychological Symptoms
Intense fear of evaluation
At the heart of social anxiety is often the fear of negative judgment: „What if I say something stupid and everyone laughs?", „What will others think of me?", „Do I seem incompetent or embarrassing? This fear can be pervasive and can relate to both concrete and hypothetical social situations.

Inner restlessness and nervousness
Many people describe an inner restlessness that is hard to tame. It's as if an alarm button is constantly being pressed, even when no specific social situation is imminent. Thoughts circle around possible risks, around what might happen, and you can't calm down.

Self-doubt and negative self-image
Social anxiety is often associated with low self-esteem. People with social anxiety may believe they are less worthy, not interesting enough, or lacking in special abilities. This negative self-image promotes the feeling of always being the „inferior" in social contexts.

Brooding and circling thoughts
Psychologically, social anxiety can lead to an endless loop of thoughts. Before an event, you may spend days thinking about everything that could go wrong. After the encounter, you replay the situation over and over in your mind, looking for mistakes or embarrassment. This rumination takes a lot of time and energy.

Avoidance behavior

A central psychological symptom is the desire to avoid anxiety-provoking situations. This may go so far as to avoid parties, family gatherings, or work events, or to cancel them in advance so as not to have to deal with the anxiety.

Fear of fear

Meta-fear is particularly insidious: the fear of your own fear. You are afraid of panicking again in a certain situation, and this scenario already triggers panic. In this way, the system builds up and intensifies the symptoms.

It should be noted that psychological symptoms often reinforce each other. Negative thoughts can trigger physical symptoms, which in turn lead to more negative thoughts („Now everyone can see me sweating!"), and so on. These vicious circles are characteristic of anxiety and can only be broken in the long term through targeted interruptions - for example, through cognitive or behavioral approaches.

Differentiation from shyness

Feeling insecure when meeting strangers is nothing to worry about at first. On the contrary, a certain amount of caution is normal and can even be helpful in new situations. But when does innocent reticence turn into a serious social anxiety disorder? Where is the line between simple shyness and a clinically relevant social phobia?

Definition of shyness

„Shy people are those who tend to be reserved when interacting with strangers or in large groups. They are reluctant to speak up, do not like to be the center of attention, and often need time to feel comfortable with new people. There are many reasons for shyness: an introverted temperament, a lack of social experience, or simply a cautious personality. The important thing to remember is that shyness is not a disease. It is one of the natural variations of the human personality. Many famous artists, scientists, and athletes were or are shy and have gone on to lead successful and fulfilling lives.

Typically, shy people do not find their behavior massively limiting. Although they may be nervous in certain situations and may need some time to gain confidence, they manage their lives without extreme psychological stress. Shyness only becomes a problem when it is so pronounced that normal social functioning is almost impossible, or when the person suffers massively. Then shyness becomes social anxiety.

Core characteristics of social anxiety

Strong and Persistent Fear

The fear of being judged or rejected by others is persistent and intense. It may occur days, weeks, or even months before a particular social event.

Distress and impairment

Social anxiety is very distressing: people feel severely restricted and avoid important social opportunities, often at the expense of friendships, career opportunities, or other areas of life. The fear is perceived as so distressing that it dominates all thoughts and actions.

Disproportionate response

The fear response is disproportionate to the actual threat. A simple conversation can feel like putting one's life in danger. Even though the mind says, „It's harmless," the body reacts extremely strongly.

Vicious Cycle of Avoidance

Avoiding social situations increases anxiety in the long run. You have fewer positive experiences, have even less confidence, and fall into a spiral that is often difficult to break out of without help.

Examples of shyness vs. social anxiety

Small talk among colleagues
Shy: The person is a little reserved at first. After a while, they thaw out and can converse normally.
Social anxiety: Intense anxiety in advance („What if they think I'm funny?"), physical symptoms (heart palpitations, sweating), and the person tries to avoid the situation or leaves in a hurry.

Lecture or presentation
Shy: Stage fright is present, you feel a little nervous, but with a little practice you can give the presentation.
Social anxiety: The anxiety can be so great that you cancel appointments or have panic attacks.

Friends and Leisure Activities
Shy: Prefers to stay in small groups, doesn't talk to strangers right away, but generally enjoys socializing.
Social anxiety: Even with friends and acquaintances, the constant fear of rejection can severely limit quality of life.

Why the distinction matters
The main reason we make such a detailed distinction here is that shyness is often considered a relatively harmless personality trait. It does not require treatment per se. Social anxiety disorder, on the other hand, usually requires targeted intervention - be it psychotherapy, a structured self-help program, or other forms of support. People who suffer from social anxiety cannot simply „let go" because the fear is deeply ingrained and accompanied by automatic, sometimes unconscious reactions.

In addition, an initial moderate level of shyness can develop over time into severe social anxiety, for example, if negative experiences or traumas are added to the mix. Therefore, it is helpful to recognize your own position on the spectrum from shyness to social phobia in order to take countermeasures in time.

How fear affects your everyday life

Social anxiety is rarely limited to a single scenario - even if it was „just" that presentation at school or work that caused you to panic. Over time, social anxiety can spread to more and more areas of your life. In this section, we will look at exactly how social anxiety can affect everyday life. We will look at aspects such as work, relationships, leisure and self-perception.

Professional challenges

Job applications and interviews

Professional situations are often highly competitive and judgmental. People who suffer from social anxiety often shy away from job interviews. It's not uncommon for highly qualified people to pass up opportunities because they don't want to go through the stress of an interview. Even if they have a job they enjoy, the anxiety of regular meetings and presentations can be so stressful that they stagnate professionally or consider quitting.

Team communication

Many jobs require teamwork, regular communication, and social skills. If you have social anxiety, even a casual conversation in the water cooler can be stressful. Meetings or brainstorming sessions can feel like an obstacle because you lack the confidence to share your ideas. As a result, people with social anxiety can quickly feel isolated or excluded in a team that relies on open communication. This, in turn, can severely limit their career advancement.

Career and self-actualization

People who are afraid to make suggestions in a meeting or say „I can do it" out loud when they are being promoted often fall short of their potential. Social anxiety can become a stumbling block when it comes to promotions, salary negotiations, or training opportunities. It is often the quiet, introverted person who does not take on a leadership role, despite their outstanding expertise, because they are afraid of the social interaction involved.

Interpersonal relationships

Partnership and Dating

Relationships are often formed through initial contact and getting to know each other. But this is where social anxiety can become a major obstacle. Flirting, first dates, and casual encounters are situations in which you are vulnerable. People who are very afraid of rejection often try to avoid these situations. This can lead to an isolation in which you crave closeness but are afraid of being disappointed or hurt.

Maintaining friendships

Social anxiety can also take a toll on existing friendships. You may cancel meetings with large groups or only show up for short periods because you feel uncomfortable in groups. Or you may be afraid to bring up problems or criticism because you're afraid your friends will reject you. In the long run, this can lead to alienation because of a lack of real closeness and openness.

Family life

People with social anxiety disorder are often tense in the family. Celebrations such as birthdays or Christmas become an ordeal. This can put a strain on family life as a whole: sometimes people with anxiety withdraw to avoid arguments or because they don't feel comfortable in large family groups. The family, in turn, feels left out and doesn't understand why you „suddenly" don't want to participate in family activities.

Leisure and everyday life

Hobbies and social groups

Clubs, classes, sports groups - they can all be great ways to meet new people and pursue your interests. However, people who are socially anxious often avoid such activities to avoid being the center of attention. Even things that are fun (e.g., dancing, singing, going on outings together) lose their appeal when the fear of embarrassment or judgment prevails.

Everyday errands

Whether it's a trip to the hairdresser, a visit to the doctor, or an impromptu chat with a neighbor, all of these situations can be uncomfortable for people with social anxiety. Some people even avoid talking on the phone, whether privately or professionally, because they feel very uncomfortable. Everyday life can become a constant stream of anxious situations if you don't learn to deal with them.

Travel and exploration

Travel and exploration, exciting and enriching for many people, can become a nightmare for people with severe social anxiety. The thought of foreign cultures, unfamiliar situations, and meeting new people on the road can be so intimidating that they choose to stay home rather than embark on an adventure. As a result, they may miss out on wonderful experiences and opportunities for personal growth.

Self-perception and identity

Because social anxiety can be so pervasive, there is often a general feeling of helplessness. People feel at the mercy of stress, unable to control their physical reactions, and experience self-doubt. This reinforces the belief that one is weak or unable to cope with life's demands.

Loss of Control and Perfectionism

Some people develop an intense perfectionism as a counter-strategy. They want to control every interaction and every word they say perfectly, lest they attract negative attention. However, life cannot be completely planned - spontaneous situations are inevitable. This striving for perfection often leads to even more pressure and fear of failure.

Negative self-talk

The stronger the social anxiety, the stronger the negative self-talk often is: „I'm boring. I'm a failure. I can't do anything right." This further lowers self-esteem. These negative beliefs act as a filter: positive external feedback is ignored or downplayed, while even the smallest insecurity is perceived as a major failure.

Conclusion: A vicious cycle in everyday life

Overall, it is clear that social anxiety can affect all areas of life. Many people do not realize until late how much they are limiting themselves, because they initially suppress some problems or adopt the attitude: „That's just the way I am, that's my character. But if you look honestly, you will see all the situations you avoid out of fear - and it often becomes clear that the price is high.

The good news is that this vicious cycle can be broken. You are not doomed to be trapped in fear forever. But in order to face it, you must first be able to recognize and name how and where it actually limits you in your daily life. This is where learning about the typical symptoms and the difference between shyness and social anxiety can help.

Self-test: Where are you right now?

Now that we have taken a closer look at the symptoms and effects of social anxiety, you may be asking yourself: „Am I really affected, and if so, how badly?" A self-test can help you make at least a rough classification. Important: This is not a professional diagnosis. Only qualified professionals (e.g. psychotherapists, psychiatrists) can make a valid diagnosis of social anxiety disorder. The test here is for self-reflection and is intended to give you clues as to what aspects you might want to look at more closely.

Below is a series of statements. Read them at your leisure and rate how much they apply to you on a scale of 0 to 4:

0 = does not apply at all
1 = rather not true
2 = partly/partly
3 = rather true
4 = completely true

It is best to write down the result for each statement and add up the points at the end.

1. I often worry about what might happen long before a social or professional event.
2. I often have physical symptoms such as sweating, palpitations or trembling when I talk to other people or in groups.
3. I avoid situations where I could be the center of attention.
4. When I have to speak in front of others, I often imagine how I might embarrass myself.
5. I believe that others usually judge me negatively (e.g. they think I am boring, strange or incompetent).

6. I often don't accept invitations to social activities because I'm too stressed.

7. After a conversation, I often mull over every word I've said for hours or days.

8. In a professional or academic context, I pass up opportunities (e.g. promotions, presentations) so as not to expose myself to social anxiety.

9. I quickly feel insecure in groups and often have the feeling that I don't belong.

10. I often feel a strong inner pressure to be perfect in social situations.

11. When I anticipate an unpleasant situation, my body immediately reacts with tension or other symptoms of stress.

12. I have the feeling that my social skills are generally not good enough.

13. I find it difficult to approach others, even when I really want to.

14. I worry about how I come across in photos or video conferences and prefer to withdraw.

15. Sometimes I am afraid that my anxiety will be visible to others (e.g. blushing, sweating, trembling) and that they will judge me for it.

Scoring

Now add up your points and read through the following categories:

0-15 points: You have no or very few signs of social anxiety. You may be a little nervous in certain situations, but this does not seem to dominate your life. This may include shyness or occasional stage fright. On the whole, however, you feel little affected by it.

16-30 points: You feel insecure and tense in certain situations. Your anxiety may not be extreme yet, but it can limit you in certain areas. Observe these situations carefully and think about what methods you can use to reduce your nervousness.

31-45 Points: You are already experiencing clear signs of social anxiety. It is likely to have a noticeable impact on your personal or professional life. In this case, it may be a good idea to learn more about the topic - for example, through self-help books (like this one), online courses, or professional support.

46-60 points: Your score indicates severe social anxiety. You are likely to avoid many situations and feel very restricted. Anxiety may dominate your daily life. It is worth seeking professional help and working on your anxiety to improve your quality of life in the long term.

This is only an initial self-assessment. Each person is unique and the exact extent of social anxiety can only be determined in a personal consultation with a professional. However, these questions provide a helpful indication of which areas of your life may be most affected.

Summary and outlook

In this chapter we looked in detail at how to recognize social anxiety in your own life. Typical physical and psychological symptoms such as heart palpitations, sweating, rumination, and avoidance were introduced and distinguished from simple shyness. We saw how far-reaching the effects can be on everyday life - from work, relationships and hobbies to general self-perception.

A key element in understanding this is the realization that social anxiety is usually more than just a little nervousness: it can be an entire pattern that profoundly affects how we think, feel, and act. At the same time, it is not simply a „weakness of character" or a „whim of the mind. It is rooted in complex contexts (Chapter 2), manifests itself in specific symptoms (Chapter 3), and-and this is the good news-can be treated with proven methods.

If you have many „aha" moments as you read, or if you recognize yourself in the symptom descriptions, it can be frightening, but also liberating: You are not alone, and there are reasons why you feel the way you do. Knowing these reasons and symptoms is the first step toward taking targeted action. In the rest of this book, you will learn strategies and techniques that can help you free yourself from the burden of social anxiety, step by step.

The next chapter focuses on the power of thoughts and feelings: How do your inner beliefs and emotional state influence your anxiety? What negative thought patterns keep it alive? And how can you actively work to break these thought patterns? This leads us into a more practical dimension, where we present concrete exercises and techniques.

Before moving on to the next chapter, take a few minutes. Make a note of the insights that were particularly relevant to you. Did you recognize symptoms that you hadn't previously seen as part of your social anxiety? Were there particular passages in the text that made you think: „This applies to me"? You may have noticed that you see certain situations in your everyday life differently now. By becoming aware of these thoughts - and ideally jotting them down in a notebook or app - you set the stage for the next step: active change.

Remember: Awareness is not an end in itself, but the starting point for setting a new course. Now that you know the areas where social anxiety is holding you back, you can look for specific ways to initiate change. Whether you do the exercises below on your own, join a support group, or work with a therapist, your newfound understanding will help you clearly communicate where exactly the problem lies.

With this knowledge, you will be well prepared to take the next step and address your inner thoughts, which is often where the roots of social anxiety lie. Get ready for an exciting journey inward - and don't forget: you're already a big step ahead once you've identified and named your fear. This is often the biggest hurdle on the road to a freer and more empowered life.

Chapter 4: The power of thoughts and feelings

In the previous chapters, you learned where social anxiety comes from and how to recognize it. You now know that factors such as biology, your family environment, and personal experiences can strongly influence how you deal with social situations. And you may have recognized yourself in some of the typical symptoms of social anxiety.

Let's take a closer look at what happens in your mind and heart when you're afraid of other people. Research consistently shows that our thoughts and feelings play a crucial role in whether and how anxiety arises and is maintained. In other words, social anxiety is not only created externally (e.g., by real negative experiences) - it is also nurtured and reinforced by our internal perceptions and processing.

This chapter is about the power of thoughts and feelings. We look at typical thought traps and how perfectionism or low self-esteem can be linked to social anxiety. Finally, we look at the moment when anxiety turns into self-criticism, a vicious cycle that often exacerbates anxiety. Again, if you understand it, you can address it. If you can see through the mechanisms behind your feelings and thoughts, it will be easier for you to find ways out and develop new, constructive patterns.

The cycle of negative thoughts

Imagine a situation where all you want to do is ask a harmless question at a meeting. But before you speak, thoughts like „What if my question sounds stupid?" or „Maybe someone will laugh because everyone already knows? Your heart starts beating faster, you feel a tingling sensation in your hands, and your mouth goes dry. You still think about saying something, but an inner voice whispers to you: „You'd better shut up before you embarrass yourself.

This voice in your head is an example of a negative automatic thought. They appear at lightning speed, often unconsciously, and have great power over your emotions and your body. If you trust them blindly, they often cause you to withdraw and avoid the situation. The brief feeling of relief („Thank God I didn't embarrass myself!") then confirms your fear: „It's a good thing I didn't say anything, this would definitely have gone wrong.

The catch is that you have no proof to the contrary. You don't know how your colleagues would have really reacted. Maybe your question would have been perfectly valid and even enriched the conversation. But as it is, you remain trapped in your negative thought pattern, and next time it will be the same - or even worse.

Understanding negative automatic thoughts

In cognitive psychology, negative automatic thoughts act as a filter through which we perceive our experiences. This filter is often based on past experiences or learned beliefs (e.g., „I'm not good enough," „Others know more than I do," „I can't express myself well"). Such beliefs act as a lens through which you color everything that happens.

Selective perception: You prefer to perceive the events that match your beliefs, e.g. a slightly bored look from a colleague, and interpret it as „he thinks my question is idiotic".

Overgeneralization: You infer a general rule from a single negative experience („I always do everything wrong!").

Catastrophizing: You immediately expect the worst („If I speak up, it will be a disaster and everyone will think I'm stupid").

These misconceptions are not only typical of social anxiety, but they also greatly exacerbate it. People who believe they will be devalued at every turn are understandably more afraid of social interactions. The problem is that negative expectations often become self-fulfilling, because you become so anxious and inhibited that the situation becomes uncomfortable - which in turn serves to confirm the negative thought pattern.

Feelings as a result of thoughts

Our feelings - whether fear, shame, insecurity, or courage - often arise in response to what we think. The same situation can therefore evoke very different feelings depending on what we think. Consider the following scene: You want to say something to a group of people, but first you have to listen quietly to what someone else is saying.

Negative thought pattern: „Everyone else is much more confident. As soon as I speak, they realize I have nothing interesting to say.

The result: You get nervous, your heart rate increases, and you feel inferior. Maybe you don't connect at all.

Constructive Thinking: „I've thought carefully about what I'm going to say, and it will be a valuable contribution. If anyone asks, I'll be happy to explain.

The result: You stay relatively calm, are curious about the group's reaction, and can express yourself more clearly.

The funny thing is that your interpretation of the situation doesn't always have to be realistic to evoke emotion. Even if the group is friendly and happy to listen to you, your belief that you are boring can make you panic.

The Vicious Cycle: Thoughts, Feelings, Behavior
Negative thought → uncomfortable feeling → unsafe behavior → bad experience → reinforcement of negative thought.

This cycle is typical of social anxiety. This is why it is so important to question the content of your thoughts and see if they are really true. Often these thoughts are exaggeratedly negative or even completely irrational. Maybe what you're trying to say is not so uninteresting, maybe the other person isn't trying to judge you at all.

One of the first steps in many therapy approaches is to keep a journal of your thoughts. By writing down what you thought in an anxiety-provoking situation, you become aware of your typical patterns. Only then can you begin to systematically change these patterns.

First exercises: Observe and reinterpret thoughts

The Thought Log: In certain situations, write down the thoughts that automatically come to mind. Try to be as honest and specific as possible. Also note the feelings that arose and how you behaved afterwards.

Reality Check: Ask yourself how realistic your fears were. Is there any evidence to the contrary? How did others react? What if the worst had happened - would it have been as catastrophic as your mind made it out to be?

Find alternative phrases: In the same situation, consciously try to find an alternative, less threatening or more constructive thought. For example, instead of thinking, „I will definitely make a fool of myself," you might think, „I have the right to speak my mind, and if I am unsure, I can say so openly.

These simple steps can help you break the cycle. Of course, deeply ingrained negative beliefs don't disappear overnight. But this kind of reflection is the first step toward lasting change.

Perfectionism and exaggerated expectations

Another important factor that promotes and perpetuates social anxiety is perfectionism. Perfectionists often set very high standards for their own behavior and fear that they will not live up to them. The result is excessive expectations that create enormous inner tension: „I have to be flawless," „I can't make any mistakes," „Every little lapse will be immediately noticed and devalued by everyone.

Why perfectionism fuels social anxiety

Perfectionism means that you believe you are only valuable or accepted if you perform flawlessly. This is particularly difficult in social situations because interactions are always somewhat unpredictable. Other people are involved and may react spontaneously, ask critical questions, or act in ways that you cannot control.

Loss of control: For perfectionists, the idea of losing control is particularly unsettling. But social situations in particular cannot be planned down to the last detail. This causes stress and anxiety.

Shame of mistakes: If you think that every little mistake is a disaster, you find it difficult to be relaxed with others. You are more concerned about not making mistakes than being open in the moment.

Avoidance and withdrawal: Because perfection is such a high standard, many perfectionists don't even try to face social challenges. They would rather cancel or withdraw than take the risk of something „not going perfectly.

Excessive expectations of oneself

Perfectionism often goes hand in hand with excessive expectations. Many people imagine that they must always appear confident, know everything, and be quick-witted at all times. But that's not true - even confident people make mistakes, get embarrassed, or have moments when they don't know what to say.

The ideal image of yourself: People who are socially anxious and perfectionistic often have an extremely high ideal in their head: „When I speak, I must be brilliant, funny, and competent. Otherwise, it's not worth saying anything.

Inner drivers: Behind this are inner beliefs such as „I must not show any weakness" or „I will only be liked if I am flawless". These beliefs drive up your anxiety levels and make you doubt yourself when things don't go well.

Self-punishment: When you don't live up to your own expectations, you may react with harsh self-criticism and shame. This leads to even more anxiety before the next social interaction.

Steps towards realistic self-assessment

The opposite of perfectionism is not „laziness" or „I don't care," but realistic self-assessment coupled with self-acceptance. Some food for thought:

Mistakes as learning opportunities

Allow yourself to make mistakes. Everyone makes mistakes, especially when they try something new. This is how you learn, grow, and gain new experiences. There is no such thing as being flawless - especially in complex social situations.

Realistic standards

Question your expectations: Are they fair? Would you hold your best friends to the same standards? We are often much harder on ourselves than we are on others.

Have the courage to be average

Sometimes it helps to consciously give 80% instead of 100%. It sounds strange, but it can be very liberating. When you realize that even „average" is appreciated by others (or doesn't stand out in a negative way), you reduce the pressure to perform.

Positive self-affirmations
If you find yourself falling back into an old pattern („I have to be perfect"), you can replace that thought with an alternative phrase, such as, „It's enough if I do it well enough. Or, „I'm okay even if I can't do everything.

Dealing with external feedback
A particular problem for perfectionists can be that they are very sensitive to external feedback. A small comment such as „You didn't express yourself clearly" is perceived as a massive judgment. In reality, constructive feedback is an opportunity to improve - it doesn't mean you're „incapable. The trick is to accept it without immediately questioning your entire self-esteem.

Gather positive feedback
It's easy to focus on what didn't go well. Pay conscious attention to compliments or where you did something well. Write them down if you have trouble remembering.

Distinguish between performance criticism and self-criticism
If someone tells you that you could present a topic more clearly next time, this is not an attack on you as a person. Try not to interpret factual feedback as a personal rejection.
Learning to settle for less than perfectionism will take pressure off you on many levels and reduce the likelihood of social anxiety. You will find that you can tolerate mistakes or inaccuracies without having your self-esteem suffer.

Self-esteem and self-acceptance

The question of perfectionism is immediately followed by the question of self-esteem. Behind the urge to be perfect is often the belief that: „I am not good enough, I have to achieve something to be loved or accepted. Weak or unstable self-esteem is an ideal breeding ground for social anxiety - because people with low self-esteem are often desperate for external validation, and at the same time fear any negative evaluation.

What is self-esteem?

Self-esteem is the basic feeling we have about ourselves: Am I happy with who I am? Or do I constantly doubt my worth and compare myself to others? People with stable self-esteem are not necessarily the „loudest" people in the room. They are often simply content with what they can and cannot do. Mistakes don't upset them immediately, and they can see criticism as a stimulus without falling into deep self-doubt.

Low self-esteem, on the other hand, manifests itself in a constant feeling of inferiority, inner self-doubt, and the feeling of having to earn one's place in society. Every social interaction becomes a test: „Am I good enough? And even the slightest negative feedback can completely shatter the fragile self-image.

The role of self-acceptance

Self-acceptance means accepting yourself with all your strengths and weaknesses. This is not the same as complacency or arrogance - because self-acceptance also means that you want to work on yourself when something is important to you. But this work is not done from an attitude of inferiority, but from a desire to grow.

For example: You notice that you get nervous in discussions. Self-acceptance means that you recognize this weakness and say:

„Okay, I'm a little reserved when there are a lot of people around. How can I still contribute without judging myself all the time?"

How Social Anxiety Can Underlie Low Self-Esteem

If your self-worth is heavily dependent on external validation, you are taking a big risk in every social interaction. Because any signal of rejection or criticism, no matter how small, can pull the rug out from under you. You are constantly on guard: „How do I look right now? Am I likable? What if someone tells me I'm talking too much or too little?

Avoidance: Fearful of having your low self-esteem confirmed, you avoid situations in which you have to prove yourself.

Overconformity: Or you try to please everyone to avoid rejection, which can lead to conflicts with your own needs.

Aggressive Defense: Some people are very sensitive to criticism and hit back verbally because they feel threatened. This can lead to physical confrontation and social isolation.

Ways to boost your self-esteem

Take time to recognize what you are good at and what you have already achieved - professionally, personally, in hobbies, or in your social circle. This will help you develop a more realistic picture of your abilities.

Mindfulness Exercises

Mindfulness means being aware of the present moment without judgment. Exercises such as meditation or breathing techniques can help you distance yourself from nagging self-doubt and see it as a „thought" rather than the truth.

Self-compassion rather than self-criticism

Try to talk to yourself as you would to a good friend. When you fail, comfort yourself instead of judging yourself. If you are nervous, accept it as a human reaction instead of branding it as a „failure.

Positive self-affirmations

Even if they sound strange at first: Saying things like „I am lovable just the way I am" or „I can make mistakes and I am still valuable" can gradually foster an inner attitude that is less dependent on external praise.

Increasing self-esteem is not a cure-all, but it is an important building block in reducing social anxiety. The more self-confidence you have, the less it will bother you when someone criticizes you or when you have to hold back in a group. You know that you are a valuable person even in those moments.

When fear turns into self-criticism

We have seen again and again in this chapter how closely thoughts, feelings and self-image are interwoven. It is particularly painful when the fear that arises in you becomes a real self-accusation. Then you don't just say to yourself: „I hope everything works out", but: „I'm so incapable. I'm embarrassing. I'm a failure."

This form of self-criticism can be worse than any real criticism from the outside, because it comes directly from yourself - and therefore appears very credible. In reality, however, it is often the product of your negative beliefs, your perfectionism and your lack of self-acceptance.

The vicious circle of self-accusation
- Anxiety occurs
- You feel the first signs of a social situation in which you are unsure. Palpitations, nervous thoughts.
- Negative interpretation
- Instead of thinking „I'm nervous, that's normal", you conclude: „Because I'm nervous, I'm weak and incapable."
- Self-accusation
- This is followed by thoughts such as „Why can't I be like everyone else?", „What's wrong with me?", „I'll never get out of this."
- Increased anxiety

This self-blame makes you feel even worse. Your self-esteem drops, your panic increases, and we are in a vicious cycle.

In the next situation, your expectation of failure becomes even greater.

The Role of Inner Criticism

Behind this dynamic is often an inner voice that you acquired in your childhood or adolescence. Perhaps you had very critical parents or were often teased at school. Sometimes we pick up such derogatory messages and turn them into our own inner critic.

The content of the critic: „You do everything wrong anyway," „Nobody likes you," „You can't do anything right," „You're ridiculous.

Intention of the critic: This part of you often tries to protect you from further rejection („If you hold back, nothing can happen to you"). But its means are devastating: it makes you small and frightens you.

When you realize that this inner critic is learned and not unchangeable, you can begin to counteract it. You can learn to uncover this voice and develop new, more constructive self-talk. It takes practice, but it is possible.

Self-compassion instead of self-accusation

To get out of this negative spiral, it is often necessary to change the self-blame into a kinder, more understanding attitude toward yourself:

Recognize the triggers

When does harsh self-criticism occur? What situations encourage it? Make a note of this to identify patterns.

Give the critic a name

Some people find it helpful to give their inner critic its own identity or voice, such as „the old nag" or „Paula the perfectionist. This makes it easier to distance yourself from these thoughts.

Ask the critic

„Is it really true that I can't do anything? Can't I do something very well?" Such questions diminish the authority of the critical voice.

Develop a Self-Compassionate Voice

Imagine how a good friend would cheer you up. How would you meet a person who was feeling the same way you are? What would you say to them? Try saying the same thing to yourself: „It's okay to be nervous, you can feel this anxiety. Everyone makes mistakes, it's part of being human".

Focus on learning opportunities

When things go wrong, ask yourself: „What can I do differently next time?" instead of „I'm a lost cause".

The difference between self-criticism and depression

Sometimes self-criticism is so strong that it takes on signs of a depressed mood or even depression. If you find yourself feeling extremely worthless for weeks at a time, barely able to enjoy activities you otherwise enjoy, and perhaps even having fears about the future or suicidal thoughts, you should definitely seek professional help.

This is because social anxiety can overlap with other mental health problems. A constant state of negative self-blame increases the risk of depression. It is important to understand that both are treatable and that you are not alone. Psychotherapists, counseling centers, or even your primary care physician may be a good place to start.

Summary and Outlook

This fourth chapter has given you an insight into the mechanisms that take place in your mind when you experience social anxiety:

Negative thoughts can lead to a rapid increase in anxiety by making us believe that we will embarrass ourselves „anyway.

Perfectionism and inflated expectations put additional pressure on us because they demand flawlessness, which is unrealistic in social situations.

Low self-esteem and a lack of self-acceptance make us dependent on external validation and increase our fear of rejection.

When all these factors come together, fear can turn into harsh self-criticism, which in turn creates a spiral of negative feelings.

The good news is that thoughts and feelings can be changed. Just as we learned certain destructive patterns, we can learn new, constructive attitudes. But it takes practice, patience, and often professional help. In the following chapters, we will look at how you can actively break this cycle by facing your fears (rather than avoiding them), through cognitive restructuring (i.e., consciously questioning and rethinking your beliefs), and through self-care (e.g., mindfulness, relaxation exercises).

You've already been given some concrete ideas: Keeping thought logs, questioning perfectionism, encouraging self-compassion, and exposing your inner critic. You can expand on these approaches in the chapters that follow. The goal is to gradually develop a new self-image that is free of fears and self-destructive patterns.

As you read this chapter, you may have thought of situations in which you felt exactly as described here. Look at these memories again. What might change in the future if you stopped believing every negative voice in your head? If you saw your nervousness as normal instead of judging yourself for it? If you allowed yourself to make mistakes without attaching your self-esteem to them?

All of these questions can help you lay the groundwork for change. Acknowledge that this is a process that won't work perfectly overnight. You may experience setbacks and fall into old thinking traps. But each moment of awareness is a step toward healing and personal growth.

In the next chapter, we look specifically at strategies and techniques that can help you manage and reduce your fears. We look at how Cognitive Behavioral Therapy (CBT) works, why exposure is so important, and how mindfulness and relaxation exercises can help. Armed with this knowledge, you will be better equipped to tackle your social anxiety and find a more positive way of dealing with yourself in the long run.

So stay tuned: the road to changing your thoughts and feelings takes work, but it's worth it. It is worth freeing yourself from unnecessary fears and living a life where you feel more confident in social relationships - and more accepting of yourself.

Chapter 5: Strategies against social anxiety

Over the past few chapters, you have gained a comprehensive understanding of the development of social anxiety, its symptoms, its causes, and most importantly, the role of your thoughts and feelings. We talked about how negative thought patterns, perfectionism, and lack of self-esteem can reinforce each other. All of this is the background to why people often get caught in a vicious cycle in which social anxiety severely limits their lives.

In this fifth chapter, we will look at specific strategies and techniques that you can use to address your social anxiety directly. These methods come from various fields of psychology and self-help. Some are very practical and action-oriented (such as exposure training), while others focus more on your inner attitude and experiencing your current feelings (such as mindfulness and meditation). Still other techniques focus on thought patterns and help you challenge your beliefs (cognitive restructuring).

It makes sense to use different approaches, especially for social anxiety, because they complement each other. Therefore, in addition to classic cognitive-behavioral therapy (CBT) and exposure training, this chapter introduces two areas that have become increasingly important in recent years: Mindfulness and meditation. These methods are now very well researched and are proving to be very helpful, especially in overcoming anxiety, because they make it possible to look at oneself more kindly and patiently and to calm the body and mind in a targeted way.

The goal of this chapter is to provide you with a versatile toolbox: You will learn how to face your fears step by step, how to stay present in difficult moments with mindfulness training, and how to calm and stabilize your mind in the long term with meditation. We will also look at other relaxation techniques and ways to integrate what you learn into your daily life for long-term benefit.

Cognitive behavioral therapy (CBT) and its principles

Cognitive behavioral therapy is one of the best-studied and most successful forms of therapy for anxiety disorders, including social anxiety. It combines two important approaches:

Behavioral therapy: looks at how your behavior is maintained and how you can change it (e.g., through exposure training, small behavioral trials, and positive reinforcement).

Cognitive therapy: Focuses on your thought patterns and beliefs. Typical negative automatic thoughts and irrational beliefs are uncovered and subjected to a reality check.

Basic assumptions of CBT

CBT assumes that your thoughts, feelings, and behaviors are interrelated. You saw this in the last chapter: Believing that you are „incapable" creates anxiety, which in turn affects your behavior (e.g., avoidance), which ultimately leads to negative experiences and reinforces the negative thoughts. This is where CBT comes in: it aims to break these vicious circles and counter them with alternative, more realistic and helpful ways of thinking and acting.

Typical methods of CBT

Thought logs: In social situations, you write down the thoughts you have, the feelings associated with them, and how you behave. This makes you aware of automated processes.

Cognitive restructuring: You learn to question negative thoughts and counter them logically. Example: „When I speak in front of a group, everyone laughs at me." → Is this really always the case? Are there any counterexamples?

Behavioral experiments: You take small steps into fear, try something new (e.g., a short conversation with a stranger), and consciously gain experiences that contradict your negative thinking.

Reward systems: You agree with yourself that you will reward yourself for progress. This reinforces positive behavior.

How CBT and mindfulness work together

In recent years, cognitive behavioral therapy has been increasingly combined with mindfulness-based approaches - so-called „third wave" methods such as Acceptance and Commitment Therapy (ACT) or Mindfulness-Based Cognitive Therapy (MBCT). These approaches integrate mindfulness exercises directly into the concept of behavioral therapy. This means that you learn not only to question your thoughts, but also to perceive them in a non-judgmental way.

This combination is particularly effective for social anxiety because we often have strong resistance to our negative feelings. When we learn to observe our anxiety without immediately reacting to it or suppressing it, we create space to try other ways of thinking and behaving. This leads us directly to the core methods we will explore in the rest of this chapter: Mindfulness and Meditation.

Facing fear step by step

Another key component of social anxiety disorder therapy is exposure. This may sound scary at first, but in practice it has proven to be one of the most effective ways to reduce anxiety in the long term.

Why exposure works

If you have social anxiety, you probably tend to avoid certain situations: These could be presentations, parties, or even everyday things like talking on the phone. But it is this avoidance that keeps the anxiety alive because you never have the chance to experience the opposite of your fears.

During exposure, you consciously place yourself in situations that trigger your fear, but you may find that the catastrophic scenario does not occur, or occurs much less frequently than you feared. In this way, your brain gradually learns that the danger is not so great. As a result, over time, you lose the ability to have a strong fear response in these situations.

Forms of exposure

Gradual exposure: You make a list of anxiety-provoking situations, rank them in order of difficulty, and tackle the easier ones first. Once you have done this, move on to the next level. Example: First you make a short phone call to a familiar person, then you call a restaurant to reserve a table, then you call a stranger at work, etc.

Systematic desensitization: Similar to gradual exposure, but combined with relaxation exercises. You learn to relax and visualize the fearful scenes in your mind. Step by step, the fear is reduced until you can face real situations.

Confrontation in vivo: Here you go directly into the real situation, without long preliminary exercises, possibly accompanied by a therapist. This is the most radical form of confrontation, which can sometimes lead to very rapid progress, but can also cause intense anxiety.

Sensual confrontation: The confrontation takes place mainly in the imagination. This can be a starting point when the „real" situation seems too stressful. Later you often move on to confrontation in vivo.

Structure of an exposure plan

Create a hierarchy of fears: List all the situations that frighten you, from the most benign to the worst-case scenario. Assign a value to each fear (0-100 points).

Define your goal: Think about what you want to achieve in the end. For example: „Be able to talk to a stranger on the phone without panicking" or „Give a short speech in front of colleagues without running away".

Step-by-step exercises: Start with a moderately anxiety-provoking situation (e.g., 30-40 points) and face it several times. Notice your physical and psychological reactions. Stay in the situation until the anxiety is noticeably reduced.

Keep an anxiety diary: Each time, note how strong your anxiety was at the beginning, how you felt, and how it changed over the course of the exercise.

Reflection and improvement: If you find that the situation is less anxiety-provoking, move up a level.

The important thing is to persist. The first few times may be uncomfortable, but the more often you dare to do it, the more you will feel your anxiety level decrease. In psychology, this effect is called habituation: your body gets used to the stimulus and reacts less strongly.

The role of mindfulness during the exposure

It is very helpful to remain mindful, especially during exposure. This means consciously focusing on the here and now: What are you feeling in your body? What thoughts are you having? What emotions are you experiencing? When you practice mindfulness, you try not to judge these phenomena, but to acknowledge them for what they are.

This may sound counterintuitive, but this is how panic can often lose its intensity. Instead of falling into the usual spiral of fear („Oh, God, I'm shaking, this is terrible!"), you might mindfully notice, „Ah, I can feel a slight tremor in my hands. That's interesting. I'm excited." This neutral stance changes your experience. You learn that although your body is showing symptoms of stress, you are not helplessly at its mercy. On the contrary, the tremor can subside if you don't fuel it with negative thoughts.

Mindfulness: consciously perceiving the moment

Now that we have seen how CBT and exposure work and where mindfulness fits in, in this sub-chapter we turn specifically to mindfulness. Mindfulness is one of the most important and influential approaches to reducing stress and anxiety in recent decades.

What is mindfulness?

Mindfulness means being aware and open in the present moment - without judgment. Instead of immediately classifying what you are experiencing as „good" or „bad", you first try to just notice it. You look at your thoughts, feelings and physical sensations as if you were discovering them for the first time.

The concept became known in the Western world primarily through Jon Kabat-Zinn, who developed the so-called MBSR program (Mindfulness-Based Stress Reduction) in the 1970s. He integrated Far Eastern meditation practices into a Western medical setting to help chronic pain patients and people with stress and anxiety disorders. Since then, mindfulness has become an integral part of the therapeutic world.

Why mindfulness helps with social anxiety

If you have social anxiety, you often tend to go to two extremes:

Past orientation: you ruminate about what „went wrong" in a conversation yesterday.

Future orientation: You imagine disaster scenarios about how embarrassing an upcoming meeting will be.

Both lead to you hardly experiencing the present moment with an open mind. Your thoughts are either in the past or the future and reinforce your negative expectations or your shame.

Mindfulness helps you to stay in the moment. You learn to bring your attention back again and again when it wanders off into thoughts of fear. In doing so, you may realize that your current reality is less dramatic than your imagination would have you believe. You also notice how your anxiety manifests itself in physical sensations - without immediately panicking because you interpret the new physical sensation as a „signal of failure".

This practice has been proven to increase your stress resilience: although you still experience unpleasant feelings, you are no longer so easily overwhelmed by them. This is particularly valuable for people with social anxiety, as they often have a high level of internal stress.

Basic techniques of mindfulness

Mindful Breathing

One of the basic exercises is to focus your attention on your breathing. Observe how the air enters through your nostrils, how your abdomen rises and falls, and how you exhale. As soon as you notice that your mind wanders, which is perfectly normal, lovingly return to your breath.

Body Scan

You mentally „walk" through your body from head to toe, noticing the sensations: pressure, heat, cold, tingling, pain, numbness. You don't try to change anything, but accept what is.

Mindful eating

In a special exercise, you can focus entirely on taste, smell and texture while eating, for example. As soon as thoughts arise, notice them and turn your attention back to the food.

Mindful walking

As you walk, you can become aware of each step you take: How do your feet land? How is your body keeping its balance? What do you feel in your legs, back, or neck?

What all of these exercises have in common is that they train your attention muscle and bring you into the here and now. Mindfulness exercises don't have to be done sitting cross-legged on a cushion - they can be integrated into your everyday life: brushing your teeth, cooking, doing the dishes.

Typical challenges

Especially in the beginning, you may feel restless or annoyed: „Why do my mind wander so much?" But the wandering isn't the problem; it's part of the practice. Every time you realize you've wandered, it's a moment of awareness. So celebrate those moments: „Ah, I've realized I've wandered - now I can come back.

Another difficulty is that people with social anxiety often suddenly notice feelings of anxiety during mindfulness practice. This can be uncomfortable because they often try to suppress their anxiety. But mindfulness also means opening up to what is. In the long run, this leads to desensitization: you learn to tolerate these feelings and let them subside on their own, rather than letting them build up again and again.

Mindfulness-Based Interventions in Practice

MBSR (Mindfulness-Based Stress Reduction): An eight-week program developed by Jon Kabat-Zinn in which you learn step-by-step mindfulness and physical exercises in a group setting.

MBCT (Mindfulness-Based Cognitive Therapy): An evolution of MBSR that incorporates more cognitive techniques. Particularly effective in preventing recurrence of depression, but also for anxiety.

ACT (Acceptance and Commitment Therapy): Focuses on acceptance of the uncontrollable and commitment to personal values. Mindfulness plays a central role.

Group classes are often appropriate for social anxiety because you learn to be mindful and share in a social setting. However, an online program or books can also be a good place to start if you are not yet comfortable in a group setting.

Meditation: finding peace within

Mindfulness and meditation are closely related, overlapping to some extent, but not identical. Mindfulness is the basic principle, meditation is often a practical method for practicing mindfulness systematically. However, there are also meditation techniques that focus less on mindfulness (in the sense of the MBSR concept) and more on other aspects (e.g. transcendental meditation, mantra meditation, etc.). In this subchapter, we will look at different forms of meditation that can help you reduce social anxiety and increase your inner stability.

What is meditation?

The word „meditation" comes from the Latin meditatio, which means „to contemplate". In Eastern traditions, however, meditation is more about letting go of discursive thinking in order to achieve a state of inner calm or clarity. In the Western world, there are now a variety of definitions, but in practice it often involves focusing the mind and developing an attitude of alertness and equanimity.

Why Meditation Helps with Social Anxiety

Stress regulation: Regular meditation has been shown to reduce stress levels by activating the parasympathetic nervous system (the „nerve of calm and relaxation") and reducing the production of stress hormones. People with social anxiety often have persistently elevated stress levels, which can be reduced through meditation.

Self-efficacy: The experience of being able to influence one's own condition through an inner exercise such as meditation (e.g., calming palpitations, reducing rumination) strengthens confidence in one's own competence. You feel less at the mercy of your fears.

Mind observation: In meditation, you learn to observe your thoughts „from the outside" rather than fully identifying with them.

This helps you realize that you are not your thoughts, and that thoughts can come and go without you having to follow them.

Different types of meditation

Mindfulness Meditation (Vipassana)

Also called insight meditation. You sit upright and focus your attention on your breath or other bodily sensations. When thoughts or feelings arise, you notice them, possibly name them („think," „feel"), and let them go without getting caught up in them.

Concentration Meditation (Samatha)

Concentration is focused on an object, such as the breath, a mantra (spoken or thought), or a candle flame. The goal is to stabilize concentration and bring the mind into a calm, focused state.

Loving kindness meditation (metta)

A special form that focuses on developing compassion and loving kindness toward oneself and others. Particularly useful for social anxiety, it can help dissolve negative self-images and develop an attitude of self-kindness.

Guided Meditations

Guided meditations in which a speaker gives specific instructions („Feel your breath, focus your attention on your heart," etc.) can be helpful for beginners. This lowers the barrier to entry because you don't have to „do" everything yourself.

Mantra Meditation

This involves repeating inwardly (or silently) a specific word or short phrase, such as Sanskrit („Om") or something personal („I am calm and serene"). This can calm the mind and have a spiritual component if you wish.

How to establish a meditation practice

Time and place
Set times and a quiet place will help you develop a routine. For example, in the morning after getting up or in the evening before going to bed. Find a comfortable place to sit (chair, pillow) and make sure you are not disturbed.

Duration
Start small: 5 minutes a day can make a big difference. Regularity is important. Slowly increase the time as you feel comfortable. Some people meditate for 20-30 minutes or more, but it depends on what works for you and what realistically fits into your life.

Posture
Ideally, you should be sitting upright, but not straining. It doesn't have to be the lotus position - a regular chair will do as long as you keep your spine straight. Your hands should be on your thighs or in your lap, and your eyes can be half or fully closed.

Deal with distractions
Turn off or mute your cell phone, and if possible, complete urgent tasks first. If a thought about the „plan for the day" comes up, acknowledge it briefly and then return to meditation.

Letting Go of Expectations
Meditation is not a method for instant euphoria. Sometimes you will be bored, sometimes something will make you nervous. This is perfectly normal. The important thing is to keep at it and trust that change will come as the weeks and months go by.

Meditation in acute situations

Although meditation is best practiced as a regular routine, you can also use it in „acute" anxiety situations - at least in a brief form. For example, if you are about to give a presentation, you can withdraw for a minute or two, close your eyes and focus your attention calmly on your breath. A few deep breaths with a slightly prolonged exhalation can calm your heartbeat and give you a feeling of serenity.

A possible mini-ritual in such an acute situation:
- Stand upright (or sit, if possible).
- Breathe in deeply, counting to 4.
- Exhale slowly while counting to 6.
- Repeat for three to five breaths.
- Briefly feel inside yourself: „How am I feeling now? Have I calmed down a bit?"

This is just a snapshot of what a deeper meditation can be, but for now, it can dampen the anxiety response and allow you to think more clearly.

Other stress management methods

In addition to mindfulness and meditation, there are a number of other relaxation techniques that can make a valuable contribution to social anxiety. They are often used in combination with CBT, exposure, or mindfulness-based approaches to specifically calm the body when it is running at full speed.

Progressive Muscle Relaxation (PMR)

Edmund Jacobson's Progressive Muscle Relaxation is a proven method in which you tense and relax individual muscle groups one at a time. This alternation teaches you to feel and release muscle tension. PMR can help achieve a state of deep relaxation, especially for social anxiety, where there is often chronic underlying tension in the body (e.g., tense neck, shaking hands).

Instructions in short form:
- Lie or sit in a comfortable position.
- Tense a muscle group (e.g. right hand and forearm) for about 5-7 seconds.
- Consciously let go and relax for 15-20 seconds.
- Systematically go through all muscle groups: Hand/forearm, upper arm, face, neck, shoulders, chest, abdomen, buttocks, thighs, calves, feet.

Breathing exercises

In addition to mindful breathing, there are special breathing techniques that you can use to activate your parasympathetic mode and reduce your physical anxiety response. One of these is the 4-7-8 method:
- Breathe in slowly for 4 seconds.
- Hold your breath for 7 seconds.
- Breathe out for 8 seconds.
- Repeat this 3-5 times.

This rhythm has a calming effect on the nervous system, as a longer exhalation stimulates the vagus nerve and can dampen the release of stress hormones.

Autogenic training

Autogenic training is a form of self-hypnosis in which you use formulaic phrases (e.g. „My right arm is getting all heavy and warm") to evoke bodily reactions that lead to deep relaxation. With a little practice, you can use this method to lower your heart rate, improve blood circulation and create a feeling of inner calm. In the case of social anxiety, this can be helpful in curbing emerging panic symptoms.

Creative relaxation methods

Visualization: You imagine a safe, pleasant place - this could be a beach, a clearing in the forest or a room where you feel safe. You bring all the details (colors, smells, sounds) to life. Such an „imaginary retreat" can quickly help you to calm down.

Music and sounds: Some people relax very well with soft music, the sounds of nature or singing bowls. Make sure that the music does not distract you, but rather carries you along.

Dance or movement: A light dance, yoga or qigong can also help you to move from your head to your body in stressful moments and release pent-up energy.

Practical tips for implementation in everyday life

Now you know a number of strategies and techniques that have been proven effective in dealing with social anxiety. But how can you incorporate them into your daily life without overwhelming yourself? Here are some specific suggestions.

Establish a routine

Structure your day: Set aside specific times for your mindfulness or meditation practice, such as in the morning after you wake up (10 minutes of mindfulness meditation) and in the evening before you go to bed (a brief body scan).

Weekly goals: On Sunday, decide what steps or exercises you would like to try in the coming week. Write them down in a small calendar or journal.

Small steps are better than no steps at all

Patience is key when dealing with social anxiety. Don't start with the most difficult exercise right away (e.g., giving a presentation in front of a large audience), but look for a moderate challenge, such as a short conversation with a colleague you barely know or a question in a meeting.

Experience shows: Each step you master gives you more confidence and takes away some of the power of fear.

Motivation and self-reward

Don't forget to praise yourself for your progress, no matter how small it may seem. The first time you manage to say something in front of a group without panicking is a major accomplishment!

You can give yourself rewards that motivate you. It doesn't have to be anything big: a relaxing bubble bath, a good movie, a meeting with a loved one. The important thing is to be aware of what you have accomplished.

View setbacks as learning opportunities

Few people manage to completely overcome their social anxiety in a few weeks. There will be days when things are better and days when you feel like you're back to square one. Try to see these setbacks not as proof of your failure, but as part of the process.

Ask yourself: „What can I learn from this situation?" Sometimes a relapse into old patterns indicates that you may have moved too fast or are under general stress. In this case, you can give yourself more time to rest or work on your strategies.

Seek support

Support groups: Especially with social anxiety, it often helps to get in touch with other people who have similar problems. You can exchange experiences and tips.

Professional support: CBT, mindfulness-based therapy, or coaching - there are many ways to get help from qualified professionals.

An integrative approach: combining techniques

The beauty of these techniques is that they can be combined. A person can do a short mindfulness meditation in the morning, use specific exposure exercises for social situations during the day, and do a progressive muscle relaxation exercise in the evening to unwind.

It is not necessary to practice all the techniques at the same time. Find what works best for you and fits into your daily routine. Many people benefit from choosing a core technique (such as mindfulness meditation) and practicing it consistently before adding other building blocks.

Long-term effects and prospects

People who regularly practice mindfulness, meditation, and other strategies can experience lasting changes in their brains over time. For example, neuroscience studies show that regular meditation practice can strengthen regions of the brain involved in emotion regulation and stress processing (such as the prefrontal cortex) while reducing the reactivity of the amygdala (fear center).

Social anxiety can gradually take control of your life. You will find that you feel more robust, less likely to panic, and increasingly able to calm yourself. This leads to more self-confidence, which in turn increases the likelihood of new positive social experiences. This can turn a vicious cycle into a virtuous one.

Better relationships and quality of life

When your anxiety is not at the forefront of your mind, you can approach relationships differently. You may have the confidence to approach others more openly, to give and receive feedback, to make new acquaintances or to deepen old ones. Feelings of „not being enough" will diminish.

This can also have far-reaching professional consequences: You may no longer have to tremble for days before a presentation, and you will be able to contribute more freely. With practice, it is quite realistic that you will realize: „Hey, not only can I keep up, I actually have something valuable to say!"

Personal growth through overcoming fear

Some people report that confronting their social anxiety gives them a whole new sense of self. They discover skills they didn't even know they had. They develop compassion - for themselves and for others - because they understand how difficult it can be to live with anxiety.

This inner maturation is a process that takes time, but it can be very rewarding. What initially seems like a heavy burden („Why do I have social anxiety?") can, over time, become a subject from which you draw strength and depth. Of course, it would be presumptuous to suggest that anxiety is exclusively positive. But in overcoming their fears, many people find access to aspects of their personality that would otherwise have remained hidden.

Frequently asked questions

Finally, we would like to address some of the questions that have arisen in connection with the techniques presented and point out possible pitfalls.

„I just can't relax."

Relaxation cannot be forced. The first step is often not to try to let go „right now," but simply to register the momentary restlessness. Mindfulness means noticing exactly what is. So when you feel that you are restless, mindfully notice it. Only from this attitude can true relaxation gradually develop.

„How long does it take for meditation to work?"

There is no general time frame. Some people feel an improvement after a few weeks of daily practice, while others take months to notice a significant change. It depends on many factors: your personality, your lifestyle, your starting point. Be patient. Remember that this is a learning process that takes place step by step.

„Is it dangerous to expose myself directly to my fear?"

Done well, exposure is not dangerous. It can be uncomfortable, that's true. But it is not dangerous in the sense that you could be seriously harmed. Your fear wants you to believe that the situation is extremely threatening, but in most cases (e.g., a conversation, a public speech) it is not a matter of life and death. It is important to take small steps and get support when needed.

„Should I even try to meditate away my fear?"

Mindfulness and meditation practices do not aim to eliminate feelings altogether. Rather, we learn to acknowledge them without letting them control us. Anxiety may not „go away" completely, but it can lose its intensity and influence. This is a more realistic goal than „I never want to feel anything again.

„What if I don't like religious or spiritual aspects?"

The beauty of mindfulness and meditation is that it can be practiced in a very secular way. Sometimes the exercises come from Buddhist or Hindu traditions, but you don't have to embrace a particular religion or spirituality to practice them. Many MBSR or MBCT courses focus exclusively on mental health and stress management.

Final thoughts: Your path is unique

This chapter has shown you that there are a variety of strategies for dealing with social anxiety. These range from cognitive behavioral therapy, which helps you break through your thought and behavioral patterns, to exposure, which is a step-by-step process of venturing into situations you have previously avoided, to mindfulness and meditation, which can bring you inner clarity and serenity. There are also various relaxation techniques that you can incorporate into your daily life.

The important thing is to find your own way. There is no „one" method that works for everyone. You may find that meditation is very good for you, while relaxation requires a lot of energy - or vice versa. After a while, you may find that you have more time for mindfulness than for daily muscle relaxation. Allow yourself to experiment.

What all methods have in common is that they require time and continuity. Social anxiety has developed and solidified over years; it doesn't go away in a few days. CBT, mindfulness, and meditation, on the other hand, offer a long-term perspective that goes far beyond overcoming anxiety: they show you ways to achieve more self-determination, empathy, and, ultimately, more joy in life.

Remember, every small change toward openness and courage is a step in the right direction. If you fail some days, that's not a bad thing. Stay curious and compassionate with yourself and you will gradually feel your social anxieties lose their hold and you will be able to create your life the way you want it to be.

You have now learned an extensive arsenal of techniques and strategies. In the next chapter, we'll look at how you can continue to build your confidence and stay on the ball so that what you've learned isn't just a flash in the pan, but becomes an integral part of your everyday life.

May you always find moments along the way when you can honestly say: „I'm nervous, but that's okay. I'm taking the next step and I'm ready to learn. This will lay the foundation for a life where social anxiety is no longer the dominant voice, but a small voice at the edge of your consciousness - and you decide how important it can be.

Chapter 6: Self-care and self-confidence

In the previous chapters, you learned about many facets of your social anxiety: its possible causes, its typical symptoms, how negative thoughts and perfectionism can perpetuate it, and specific strategies-from cognitive behavioral therapy and exposure to mindfulness and meditation-that can help you overcome it. But while managing anxiety is an essential part of the process, it doesn't stop there. It is equally important to nurture and strengthen your own resources and self-esteem. This is the only way to ensure your success in the long run and to create a stable basis for facing new challenges more calmly.

This is exactly what this sixth chapter is about: self-care and self-confidence are the two pillars on which you can build your life if you no longer want to let social anxiety rule your life. We will look at how to discover and activate your resources (skills, strengths, interests), which positive beliefs can help you change your self-image, how to deal constructively with setbacks, and why it is important to stick with it for the long haul in order to consolidate successes. Throughout, we will draw on the lessons learned in the previous chapters, because self-care and self-confidence are not isolated topics; they are closely related to all the strategies and techniques discussed in the previous chapters.

Discover resources

Why Resource Orientation Matters

The early chapters often deal with problems: fears, insecurities, negative thoughts. This is a necessary step in understanding where these problems come from and how they manifest. However, it is just as important to focus on your positive aspects, your strengths, talents, and interests. In psychology, this is called „resource orientation": instead of looking only at weaknesses and deficits, we consciously ask: what does the person already have that can help him achieve his goals and improve his outlook on life?

This can be a salutary change of perspective, especially in the case of social anxiety. For years, many sufferers have focused primarily on their perceived deficits: „I'm too quiet," „I'm not good at talking," „I don't have anything interesting to say." The positive aspects - „I am a good listener," „I am reliable," „I have an eye for detail" - are overlooked or dismissed. This leads to a distorted self-perception in which self-esteem is further eroded.

A resource-oriented attitude seeks to redress this imbalance. It is not about denying weaknesses or sweeping problems under the rug, but about expanding awareness: you are more than your fears, more than your insecurities. You have skills and qualities that are valuable to your life and that can be strengthened now.

Methods for Discovering Resources

The first step in discovering your resources is self-reflection and openness. A few questions can help guide you:

What do I like to do?

Take a look at your hobbies, interests, or daily activities that make you feel good and give you energy. Perhaps you enjoy cooking, photography, gardening, or playing an instrument.

When am I in flow?

The flow state occurs when we are completely absorbed in an activity, lose track of time, and feel competent. When was the last time you felt this way? What were you doing?

When I look back on my life, what am I proud of?

It could be a high school diploma, a successful presentation, a good group of friends, or even a small everyday act of heroism such as helping someone in need.

What do others value about me?

Ask friends and acquaintances what they like about you. Often others see our strengths more clearly than we do. They may praise your patience, sense of humor, or organizational skills.

What helped me in the crisis?

Look at situations in your life that have been difficult. What helped you then - inner strengths, special skills, a creative hobby, close friendships? All of these things can be helpful today.

A proven exercise is the resource interview: Ask someone to „interview" you for half an hour on topics such as „What have you already mastered?", „What skills have helped you?" or „Where have you grown? Make a note of what comes up. You may be surprised at how many strengths come to light when you work hard.

Tools: Strengths and Interests Lists

To make your resources more tangible, you can make a list of strengths. Write down all the positive qualities and skills you can think of. Take your time and add to the list over the next few weeks. Typical strengths might include
- Strong communication skills (even if you have social anxiety, you may be able to communicate very well in writing or be helpful in one-on-one situations).
- Empathy and listening skills.
- Creativity and innovation.
- Organizational skills.
- Perseverance and discipline (e.g., you have completed an apprenticeship or course of study despite many hurdles).
- A sense of humor and the ability to lift the spirits of others.
- Curiosity and a willingness to learn.
- An eye for aesthetics (maybe you like to design rooms or are good at drawing).

You can also make a list of your interests: What are you passionate about? Sports, technology, music, nature, politics, animal rights, literature? Sometimes we neglect our interests, especially when social anxieties hold us back (e.g., we don't join a club because we're afraid of groups). Yet these interests can be the key to a more fulfilling life and positive social experiences.

Learning to manage hidden strengths

Some people feel they have strengths but are afraid to show them because they think they will attract negative attention or be criticized. In the case of social anxiety, perhaps you have a great voice and would love to sing, but are afraid to perform in front of even one person. Or you may be great at drawing, but are ashamed to show it because you feel unworthy.

In such cases, it helps to take small steps, perhaps starting by showing something to a good friend, getting feedback, and gradually expanding your comfort zone. This comes full circle to the exposure in chapter five: allowing your strengths to become visible gradually, which in turn can give you a sense of accomplishment.

Resource orientation and self-care

Knowing your resources is an important part of self-care. Only when you know what is good for you and what you are good at can you use these resources to stabilize and nourish yourself. For example, if you find that playing music or dancing strengthens you, you can consciously use it as a counterbalance to a stressful social situation - as a kind of „energy kick" for your self-esteem.

Establish positive beliefs

The power of our convictions

From the previous chapters, you already know how negative and destructive some beliefs can be-for example, „I am not interesting" or „I can never make mistakes. These beliefs trap you in fear. So it makes sense that you can counter them with positive beliefs that match the new image you want to have of yourself and the world.

Positive beliefs do not mean denying reality or convincing yourself that you are „superhuman. Rather, it is about formulating realistic and expanded beliefs that are less restrictive and destructive and that help you feel freer and more courageous in social situations. Examples include

- „It's okay to be nervous. I can still contribute."
- I don't have to be perfect to be accepted.
- My opinion has value, even if not everyone shares it.
- „I can make mistakes and grow from them."
- Even if some people don't like me, I can like myself.

Detect and transform negative beliefs

A sensible first step is to become aware of your negative beliefs. They are often so automatic and unconscious that you hardly notice them. However, you may feel them in the form of fear, shame or self-deprecation as soon as you get into a social situation. Write them down. Typical examples of social anxiety:

- „Everyone else is more confident than me."
- „I'm guaranteed to make a fool of myself if I say anything."
- „I'm boring, nobody is interested in me."
- „I can only show who I am if I'm 100% sure that I come across as great."

Think about how you can change each of these sentences into a more positive, constructive form that is credible to you. Example: „Everyone else is more confident" could become: „Some people seem confident, but they also have insecurities. I can feel my way forward step by step and have just as much right to take my place."

It's important to choose sentences that don't sound like pure fantasy. „I am the greatest!", for example, would be an exaggeration if you experience yourself as an anxious person. Instead, choose phrases that make you realize: „That could be true if I let it be."

Anchoring positive beliefs in everyday life

Writing down positive beliefs is a good start, but they also need to be internalized. The following techniques may help:

Affirmation Cards

Write your positive beliefs on cards or sticky notes and place them in places where you see them often: on your mirror, on your desk, in your purse. Each time you see them, read them out loud or repeat them to yourself.

Link to posture
Some people find it helpful to consciously adopt a supportive posture while saying the affirmations, such as standing up straight, shoulders back, looking straight ahead. This sends a nonverbal signal to the brain: „I am in my power.

Visualize
When you say: „I am allowed to speak my mind even when I am nervous," imagine a specific situation in which you are doing just that: speaking to a group in a calm, perhaps slightly excited, but steady voice. Imagine how you feel as you live this new belief.

Daily Ritual
Consciously take 5 minutes in the morning or evening to go through your beliefs and feel how they make you feel. This is a small but powerful ritual for reprogramming your mind.

Typical hurdles when practicing new beliefs

Resistance: You may feel inner voices saying: „That's not true! You're still a failure!" This is normal. These voices of resistance are part of your old belief system. Let them be without giving them too much power.

Impatience: You want to move forward quickly, but your old beliefs have become entrenched over many years. Take your time.

Falling back into old patterns: When you experience stress or setbacks, it's easy to fall into the „I'm just not capable" pattern. This is when it helps to consciously return to your positive affirmations and say: „I can have this crisis and still believe in myself.

The Power of Positive Beliefs in Everyday Life
As your new beliefs begin to take hold, you will find that they give you more peace in typical everyday situations. You may still feel nervous about giving a presentation, but your new beliefs will

whisper to you: „I can do this, nervousness is part of it, and it's okay if I'm not perfect. This makes it easier for you to access your resources (Chapter 6.1) because you are less in your own way and can use your skills more freely.

Dealing with setbacks

Why setbacks are normal

Working on your social anxiety and self-confidence is a process that happens in waves. It's almost impossible for everything to go perfectly from one day to the next or for you to never experience anxious or depressed phases again after your initial successes. Setbacks are not only normal, they can even be an important part of your personal growth.

Setbacks often occur when you take on a new challenge or when external stress factors (e.g. a demanding job, family problems, health problems) come into play. Perhaps you have just felt confident enough to master an important social situation and suddenly something goes wrong or the old fear returns.

Typical forms of setbacks

The avoidance behavior returns.

You have made an effort to practice facing the fear, and suddenly you find yourself turning down invitations to avoid stress again.

Negative Self-Talk

You really wanted to hold on to your positive beliefs, but in a stressful situation your mind starts to say: „You'll never make it, it's no good, you're a lost cause.

Physical symptoms of anxiety

You may have gotten better at controlling your heart palpitations and trembling, but now they are back with a vengeance.

Failure in a particular situation

You dared to give a speech and it didn't go well - you stumbled or couldn't express your thoughts clearly. This feels like „proof" of your incompetence.

Strategies for overcoming setbacks

Accept

First, it is helpful to acknowledge the setback without immediately falling into self-blame. The inner attitude might be: „Okay, it's been a stressful day, I've fallen back into old patterns. It's not nice, but it's part of the game.

Reflection

Think about what happened. Was there a particular trigger? Were you stressed, tired, sick? Were you neglecting your mindfulness or meditation practice? In what situations were you more uncertain than usual - and why?

Build on successes

Be aware of the progress you have already made. You may have proven many times that you can overcome challenges. One failure or one bad day will not undo those experiences.

Timely support

If you find yourself in a downward spiral, talk to someone you trust or a therapist. Sometimes even a short conversation can help put the situation into perspective.

Make new action plans
You can often learn from setbacks. You may realize that it would have been better to take things one step at a time, or that you were taking on too much. Adjust your goals instead of giving up completely.

Building resilience - the art of coming back strong

Resilience means „getting back on your feet" after difficulties. It is not about not experiencing any more crises, but about emerging positively from them. Every setback you experience and analyze makes you more resilient. You learn that you can endure crises and doubts without being permanently broken by them.

Practical tips to strengthen your resilience:
- Keep a diary: Don't just write down problems, but also your reactions and insights. Over time, you will see a pattern of how you overcome crises.
- Self-care on winding days: If you feel that you are more inse cure, allow yourself time for mindfulness exercises, a walk, a warm bath or other beneficial activities.
- Small pleasures in everyday life: Create small islands of joy (such as a special cup of tea, doing something creative, listening to a favorite song). This can alleviate the frustration of a setback.
- Community: Keep in touch with people who are good for you. Maybe join a self-help group or talk to other sufferers online.

See setbacks as a „training partner"

Try to see setbacks as an opportunity to apply what you have learned and to strengthen yourself internally. If you manage to stay true to yourself during a difficult phase and don't throw everything away, your self-confidence will grow enormously. You realize: „I'm stronger than I thought. Even if I fall down, I can get up again. It is precisely this self-confidence that gives you security for future situations.

Stick with it in the long term and consolidate successes

The Importance of Continuity

Developing new attitudes and behaviors is not a project that can be „done" in a few weeks. Fears and old beliefs can be very persistent. That's why you need continuity to make long-term changes. You have been introduced to many methods: mindfulness, meditation, exposure, cognitive restructuring, relaxation exercises, resource orientation. They are all process tools. They unfold their full power when you use them repeatedly, preferably daily or at least several times a week.

Think of it like learning to play a musical instrument: Only those who practice regularly make progress. And just like playing music, there will be times when you don't feel like it, or you don't have much time, and you realize you're getting a little rusty. But as soon as you start practicing hard again, your skills will come back - often faster than you think. It's the same with mindfulness and all the other tools.

Your personal toolbox

It's best to build a toolbox that you can use when you need it. For example, write down
- Short mindfulness exercises (1-5 minutes): e.g. breath observation, body scan light, grateful gazing at the sky.
- Longer meditation or relaxation sessions (10-30 minutes): e.g. guided meditation, progressive muscle relaxation, autogenic training.
- Exposure steps (if still relevant): e.g. weekly task of making small talk with a stranger or giving a short presentation as part of a team.
- Positive beliefs: A list of your most important affirmations to remind yourself of in difficult moments.
- Resilience Boosters: Things that immediately make you feel better, such as music, dancing, going for a walk, writing in your journal, talking to a specific friend on the phone.

You can organize this „toolbox" in a note-taking app or on paper so that you can refer to it at any time-especially in moments when you feel that „fear is coming back: „The fear is coming back" or „I'm losing confidence in myself.

Measuring success - but how?

Naturally, you want to know if you are making progress. With social anxiety, this is not so easy because progress is often subtle or because we focus on the failures. Here are some suggestions for measuring your progress:

Journal: Write about how you felt in social situations, what symptoms you experienced, and what techniques you used. Compare your entries periodically.

Scales: Rate your anxiety in a situation on a scale of 0 to 10. If you notice that you used to be an 8 and now you are a 5, this is significant progress.

Define goals: Set specific and achievable goals. For example: „In two months, I want to be able to speak in front of a group without panicking. If you achieve this goal, you can consider it a success.

Outside feedback

It can be helpful to ask friends or family for feedback. Often, others will notice that you seem more relaxed and confident before you realize it. However, be wary of anyone criticizing or putting you down. They should be people who can support and encourage you without giving you false compliments.

Celebrate your successes

A common problem with people with social anxiety is that they are quick to dismiss or minimize successes: „That was nothing special." But this is a missed opportunity to build confidence. Every success, no matter how small - a successful date, a frank word in a team meeting that you wouldn't have dared say before - deserves to be acknowledged.

You could start a little ritual: Write down your successes (preferably right after you experience them) on a piece of paper or in a book; call it your „success diary. Once a week, take a look at what went well. Not only will this lift your spirits, but it will also help you objectively document that change is actually happening.

Conclusion: A stable path to self-care

In this sixth chapter, we have explored the topics of self-care and self-confidence. It has become clear that social anxiety does not disappear simply by „training" it away, but that we must also focus on the positive side of our personality and our potential. To summarize the most important points

You are more than your fear. Your strengths, interests, and abilities are treasures to build upon. By recognizing and activating them, you create a solid foundation for positive experiences and self-affirmation.

Negative thinking can be replaced with realistic and constructive beliefs. This requires regular practice and a willingness to contradict old patterns. Think about affirmations, anchor them in your daily life and experience how they change your actions.

Setbacks or periods of decline are normal. They do not mean that you are „incapable," but are part of a learning and growth process. It is important that you reflect on your setbacks, learn from them, and not become discouraged.

The methods from the previous chapters will only have a lasting effect if you use them continuously. Mindfulness, exposure, cognitive restructuring, and any other strategies should become an integral part of your daily or weekly routine.

Self-care also means giving yourself credit for everything you accomplish. Every success, no matter how small, is a step in the right direction and deserves to be recognized and celebrated.

As you continue on this path, a new attitude will gradually develop: Confidence that you can overcome challenges, that you are not alone in your anxiety, and that you can draw on your strengths even in difficult times. Social anxiety will have less and less power over your life. It may still be noticeable in some situations, but it no longer defines who you are and how you should behave.

With this chapter, you have reached an important milestone: you have not only dealt with your fears, but you have also discovered the positive side of yourself. The next step is to further strengthen your communication and social skills: How can you put your new insights into practice in your interpersonal interactions? What types of communication and skills will enhance your well-being and self-confidence? This is the subject of Chapter Seven, in which we look at specific communication techniques and social skills - so that you can develop your growing confidence in relationships and conversations in a very practical way.

Until then, take a moment to hug yourself - mentally or physically. You are in the midst of a process of change that requires courage, patience, and perseverance. And every step you take is a valuable step toward a life in which social fears no longer define your boundaries, but you can choose how you want to move in the world.

Keep at it - with self-care, self-confidence, and the constant awareness that you have valuable resources within you that are just waiting to support you.

Chapter 7: Communication and social skills

So far in this book, you have explored what social anxiety is, where it comes from, and how you can overcome it using various techniques (exposure, mindfulness, meditation, cognitive restructuring, etc.). You have also learned the importance of self-care, self-confidence, and discovering your resources to create a stable foundation for your personal development.

But how can all this be applied to communicating with other people? After all, we don't just face social challenges in our own minds, but also very concretely in conversations, discussions, when meeting new people, or when dealing with conflict. This is where the seventh chapter comes in: It focuses on communication and social skills, especially conflict resolution, networking, and small talk. These three areas are crucial not only for our professional development, but also for building and maintaining stable social contacts and relationships.

Contrary to popular belief, conflict is not always destructive: if handled correctly, it can promote growth and openness. Networking is much more than a „career machine" - it can also be a tool for building inspiring and supportive relationships that enrich your life. And even the sometimes ridiculed small talk can pave the way for breaking down initial barriers and engaging in real exchange.

These are all areas that people with social anxiety often avoid or find particularly threatening. In this chapter, you will learn how to deal with conflict constructively, how to be more confident when networking, and how to see small talk as an opportunity rather than a burden. We build on the previous chapters because one thing is clear: communication works best from a place of increased self-awareness and a certain composure in the face of your own (and others') insecurities.

The basics of successful communication

Before we get into the specifics of conflict resolution, networking, and small talk, let's take a quick look at the basics of successful communication. After all, it doesn't matter if you're trying to resolve a dispute or build a new professional network: Communication is always a two-way process in which we not only speak, but also listen, observe, interpret, and adapt to each other.

Active listening

„Active listening means listening to the other person with full attention, not just half an ear. This includes

Physical presence
Look at the person you're talking to (but don't stare), turn to them, nod occasionally, or use facial expressions and gestures to show you're listening.

Verbal signals
Short affirmations („Yes," „Hm," „I see") can make you feel heard. It is important to use them appropriately and not excessively.

Paraphrasing
Summarizing what the other person has said in your own words can help avoid misunderstandings. For example: „If I've understood you correctly, do you think the new distribution of tasks is unfair because you now have to work more hours per week?"

Ask questions
Show genuine interest by asking questions when you want to know more about something or when you feel the other person

would benefit from a deeper understanding („Can you tell me more about that?").

Active listening is a valuable skill, especially for people with social anxiety, because it allows you to focus less on your own stage fright and more on what the other person is actually saying. This takes the pressure off you - you don't have to think about what you're going to say next, but you can actually engage with what's being said.

Self-revelation and authenticity

While active listening shows that you are open to the other person, self-disclosure is also an important aspect of successful communication. This means that you don't hide yourself completely, but also reveal something about yourself. This does not mean that you reveal your most intimate secrets right from the first contact. But it can mean that you openly express your attitudes, feelings or thoughts on a topic instead of just nodding your head evasively.

This is particularly challenging when it comes to social anxiety: it can be scary to „show yourself". But authenticity creates trust and helps to deepen relationships. Many people find it very likeable and disarming when someone doesn't maintain the perfect façade but instead admits their insecurities. Finding the right balance - being open enough without feeling uncomfortable - is a process. With practice and sensitivity, it can be achieved step by step.

Body language and non-verbal signals
In addition to what we say, we always communicate through our body language:
- Eye contact: A brief, open look signals interest and
  friendliness. Staring too fixedly comes across as creepy; not

making eye contact at all can come across as insecure or dismissive.

- Posture: Stand or sit upright but relaxed, shoulders not cramped upwards, upper body slightly turned towards the other person.
- Facial expressions: A smile in the right place, an open facial expression that shows that you empathize or think along with them.
- Gestures: Restrained, but not completely rigid gestures, exaggerated gestures can appear hectic, while no movement at all can convey a defensive attitude.

People with social anxiety sometimes tend to use very restricted body language out of insecurity: crossed arms, slumped shoulders, downward gaze. It can help to consciously train yourself to adopt a constructive posture, even if it is unfamiliar at first.

The interplay of giving and receiving

Successful communication is a matter of giving and receiving. Think of it as two people rolling a big ball around together: One person pushes the ball a little, the other catches it and pushes it further. It's similar in a conversation: sometimes you talk (send), sometimes you listen (receive). In a good conversation, this is balanced. Make sure you give the other person space, but also take space when you need to share.

Conflict resolution: arguing constructively and setting boundaries

Dealing with conflict is a particularly challenging area of communication. Socially anxious people often tend towards avoidance: they prefer to swallow anger or dissatisfaction rather than risk a potential conflict. This may keep the peace in the short term, but in the long term it often leads to frustration, misunderstandings or even broken relationships.

Wherever people come together, there are different interests, values or approaches. Dealing constructively with conflict does not mean avoiding every argument, but rather managing disputes in such a way that everyone involved can learn from them and find a common solution.

Understanding conflict: Where is the root?

Before actively tackling a conflict, it is helpful to analyze what it is actually about. Is it a purely factual problem (e.g. differing views on the best approach to a project)? Or are there deeper feelings behind it, such as resentment, jealousy or old injuries?

Factual conflicts: A solution can often be found by arguing clearly and checking the facts together.

Relationship conflicts: These are about personal needs, respect, trust, closeness or distance. Such conflicts can require intensive discussions in which feelings play a central role.

Sometimes factual and relationship conflicts become intertwined. It is then all the more important to clarify what needs to be dealt with and at what level.

Clarify your own attitude

Approaching conflicts constructively requires inner stability - especially in the case of social anxiety, where the thought of con-

frontation quickly triggers panic. One way to help is to ask yourself in advance:
- What do I need in this conflict? (e.g. clarity, respect, apology, compromise, equality)
- What am I prepared to give? (e.g. understanding, time, willingness to compromise)
- What boundaries are important to me? (e.g. I do not accept personal attacks or insults)

Be aware that conflict resolution is a process in which both sides bear responsibility. If you put yourself in the role of victim from the outset („I'm too shy anyway, I have nothing to say"), you are preventing a fair discussion. Conversely, if the other person has a completely different position and is not prepared to listen, a constructive dialog is not possible in the first place. You should also acknowledge this to avoid wasting energy unnecessarily.

Non-violent communication according to Marshall Rosenberg

One of the best-known approaches for constructive conflict discussions is non-violent communication (NVC). It is based on four steps:
1. observation: describe the situation without judging: „Last week, you canceled our appointment twice, each time on the same day."
2. feeling: Share how you feel about it: „I felt disappointed and hurt."
3. Need: State the underlying need: „Reliability is important to me in order to feel safe and valued."
4. Request: Formulate a specific request: „Would you be willing to let me know sooner if something changes with you so that I can plan accordingly?"

This model helps to leave the level of accusations and reproaches behind and focus on feelings and needs. This can also be very helpful with social anxiety, as you don't have to fight, but can communicate your perspective clearly and calmly.

Setting Boundaries and Saying No

Conflicts often arise when people fail to communicate their own boundaries in a timely manner. People with social anxiety often swallow discomfort until it erupts in anger or sudden withdrawal. However, it is much more effective (and easier for the other person to understand) to say „no" or „not like that" in a timely manner.

- Use plain language instead of excuses: Instead of making up a crude excuse, say: „I'm not feeling well today, so I'd like to go home.

- Be short and polite: A straightforward „I'm afraid I can't help this weekend because I have other commitments" is better than a rambling „Maybe it'll work out, let's see...".

- Offer alternatives: When you say „no," sometimes you can offer an alternative. For example: „I can't help you on Sunday, but maybe I have two hours one night a week to help you."

The beauty of clear boundaries is that you will find that many people will respect them - and even take you more seriously. Of course, it may happen that someone reacts angrily. But that's less your fault than the other person's. Growing from this is part of overcoming fear: You learn to stand up for your needs and experience that you can get through it unscathed.

Conflict Resolution for Chronic Avoidance

If you find that you are systematically avoiding conflict, it can be helpful to make a small plan:
- Identify a „small" conflict (e.g., someone lent you a book that is now badly damaged and you are unhappy with how they handled it).
- Formulate an „I" message (e.g., „I was upset because the book is very important to me. I would like you to consider this in the future before returning it to me").
- Communicate this clearly and objectively, without accusation.
- Observe your fear: You will probably feel your heart pounding - stay calm and breathe.
- Wait to see how the other person reacts. They may be surprised, apologize, offer a replacement... The reaction is often less negative than your fear predicts.

Once this has worked, you can gradually move on to larger conflicts. As with exposure, you learn that direct communication and confrontation leads to less stress in the long run, even if it is uncomfortable in the short run.

Master Networking

For many people, networking conjures up images of standing receptions, business cards, and superficial small talk. Especially for people who suffer from social anxiety, networking often feels artificial or forced, and the idea of approaching strangers can be downright panic-inducing. At the same time, we know that networking can open doors both professionally and personally, and is often more important than professional competence alone.

But networking doesn't have to be an obsession. It can be about meeting interesting people, discussing common interests, learning from each other, and supporting each other. So how can you use networking to your advantage without becoming a slave to it?

The mindset of networking
The first step is to examine your attitude toward networking. If you're thinking, „I have to play up to complete strangers just to get something out of it," that's uncomfortable - and it blocks you. Instead, think of networking as an
- exchange: you give and you get. It's about mutual interest.
- Focus on topics and industries: Instead of collecting contacts randomly, focus on areas and people that really interest you.
- Maintain long-term relationships: Networking is not „business card here, business card there," but can develop over weeks, months, and years.

Above all, be curious about people. Remember that even the most successful person in business was once a beginner or had personal problems. If you show genuine interest, a natural flow of conversation will often develop.

Possible places and opportunities for networking include
   - Professional events: trade shows, conferences, seminars. You will automatically meet people in your field.
   - Workshops and courses: If you attend a training seminar, you will meet like-minded people. Common interests are a good icebreaker.
   - Online platforms: Networking sites such as LinkedIn, Xing, or professional forums are great places to talk about interests and projects before you meet in person.
   - Leisure and volunteering: Don't underestimate this: Networking can also take place in a club, a civic group or through a shared hobby - often in a very uncomplicated way.

First contacts for the socially anxious
A simple way to get started is to ask about the person's area of expertise or current project („What do you do for a living?" or „What are you working on right now?"). Most people enjoy talking about their work.

Show interest: Ask open-ended questions to get the other person talking. („How did you get into it?", „What fascinates you most about it?").

Own relevance: When appropriate, mention your connection to the topic („I'm also interested in XY because...").

Time limit: If you are very nervous, plan to talk in small chunks. You don't have to talk for hours. After a few minutes, say: „Thanks for the nice conversation, I'm going to look around. Maybe I'll see you later.

Exchange your contact information: If the conversation goes well, ask nicely if you can network on LinkedIn or get an email address.

Over time, you will become more confident: eventually, you may even be able to take the initiative and actively approach a person you find interesting. Remember: Many people are happy to receive genuine interest and are glad not to be sitting alone in a corner.

Maintain your network

Once established, contacts are only worth something if they are nurtured. This does not mean that you have to reach out every week. But a short message every now and then („How are you?", „I just read an interesting article on topic XY that might interest you") shows that you are thinking about the person. Even if you only send a little sign of life every few months, the contact stays alive.

Especially for people with social anxiety, this step is sometimes easier because it can be done in writing - via email, Messenger, or LinkedIn message. Small hints that you are there and interested in the other person are a wonderful way to avoid the fear of direct confrontation without remaining passive.

A well-established network can open doors not only professionally, but also personally. You can find people who share your interests and values, make friends, receive invitations to exciting events, and exchange ideas during challenging times. Networking can be an emotional support when it is based on genuine exchange and mutual goodwill - not just a calculation of what you can get.

Master small talk

Finally, we turn our attention to a topic that is a major hurdle for many people with social anxiety: Small talk. This short, superficial conversation when first meeting someone or in waiting situations (in the elevator, at the reception desk, during a coffee break) can make anyone feel insecure: „What am I supposed to say?", „I don't have anything interesting to say!", „What if it gets awkwardly quiet?

Yet small talk plays a central role in everyday social life. It is the lubricant between strangers who want to make polite conversation without getting into intimate topics. If you learn to feel more comfortable in this seemingly banal setting, it is often much easier to start more in-depth conversations.

The purpose of small talk
Small talk is often criticized for being „superficial. But it serves important functions:

Establish contact: Instead of asking direct personal questions, you can first gauge the atmosphere: „How is the mood?", „Does the other person have a sense of humor?

Create a comfort zone: Using innocuous topics (the weather, an event, a trip) establishes some common ground. Both parties can feel confident that the conversation won't get too personal.

Transition to deeper topics: It often happens that a casual introduction turns into an intense exchange: „Oh, you play guitar too? How did you get started?"

Typical Small Talk Topics
Weather: Classic, sounds trite, but can be a door opener.
Current events: „How do you like the conference so far?", „Did it take you long to get here?"
Setting: „The building is impressive - do you know when it was built?"
Common acquaintance: „I heard that you also know XY. Where from?"
Personal: Hobbies, favorite restaurants, vacation plans, sports. Don't get too intimate or bring up sensitive topics (politics, religion) - unless you sense that the other person is genuinely interested.

Successful small talk strategies
Take a Deep Breath: Before you start talking to or being approached by someone, consciously take a deep breath. This reduces initial panic.
Ask open-ended questions: Instead of yes/no questions. „What is your favorite part of the event so far?" opens up more conversation than „Did you like it?
Respond to what the other person says: If the other person talks about the traffic jam, you can ask if he or she often drives, if there are alternatives, etc. This shows genuine interest. This shows genuine interest.
Interject personal details: Don't be afraid to interject your own opinion or a little anecdote („I've been riding my bike more lately because..."). This makes the conversation seem more authentic and less like a question-and-answer game.
Have emergency topics ready: If you can't think of anything, have a few neutral topics ready (e.g., an interesting movie, an interesting article, a funny anecdote from the ride). You don't have to be funny right away, but an anecdote or two will help fill in the blanks.

When the conversation stalls

It's normal for small talk to fall flat at times. The chemistry is not always there. It doesn't mean you've failed. You can say goodbye in a friendly way and say you're going to look around („It was nice chatting with you. I'll see who else is here"). This is perfectly legitimate and will rarely be perceived as rude if you say it with a smile and a grateful tone.

Moving from small talk to a deeper exchange

Sometimes small talk develops into a real conversation. You can tell when the other person is asking questions, sharing personal things, or showing genuine interest. Don't be afraid to use this moment to become more open. You can then calmly say: „It's exciting that you're thinking about this - tell me more about it. This shows that small talk is not an end in itself, but a door opener to a more human and deeper dialogue.

Summary and outlook

In this chapter, you have learned how diverse and fascinating the field of communication and social skills can be-especially for people with social anxiety, who are often forced into a passive role. You have learned that
Conflict is not inherently negative, but an opportunity for clarification and growth. With clear communication (nonviolent communication, I-messages) and the courage to set boundaries, you can foster respect and understanding.

Networking doesn't have to be a chore. If you are interested in topics and people and dare to take small steps, you can make valuable contacts that go beyond the purely professional.

Small talk is not irrelevant chitchat, but an important social tool for building initial bridges and breaking the ice. With a little preparation, a few neutral topics, and a genuine interest in the other person, it's not difficult to make small talk.

All of these points build on what you have learned in the previous chapters: Mindfulness (Chapter 5) will help you not to panic. Self-care and self-confidence (Chapter 6) are crucial to feeling strong enough inside to actively engage in communication. And of course, methods such as exposure, relaxation, and cognitive restructuring can help you step out of your comfort zone.

Be aware that communication skills, like mastering a musical instrument or a foreign language, require practice. You won't become the perfect conflict manager, networker, or small-talk ace overnight. But every little step makes a difference: the first time you speak up in a conflict, the first time you approach someone proactively, or the moment you really start chatting in small talk without thinking about your fear the whole time.

In Chapter Eight, you will learn how to get outside support, whether from family, friends, professionals, or a community of sufferers. After all, no one has to overcome social anxiety alone.

Communication is a process that takes place not only within ourselves, but also in our relationships with other people. And it is often in these relationships that we find the strength and security we need to free ourselves permanently from excessive anxiety.

So take away from this chapter the certainty that you can make real progress not in spite of your sensitivity, but because of it. A sensitive and mindful approach to conflict, networking, and small talk can open doors for you that you didn't even know existed. Your own personal communication journey begins now - or may have already begun.

May each conversation bring you new insights and contacts, and prove to you that you can do more than you sometimes think.

Chapter 8: Finding support

Over the past few chapters, we have looked in detail at how social anxiety develops, how to recognize it, and strategies for overcoming it. We've talked about cognitive techniques, mindfulness and relaxation techniques, self-care, and the importance of social communication. Despite all these helpful methods, you may still feel overwhelmed or alone at certain times in your life. You may need additional support in addition to your own commitment to make real progress.

This is where this chapter comes in: „Finding Support. It looks at how to involve those around you, what professional help is available, and how to connect with peers or mentors. We also look at how community activities and a supportive network can reduce feelings of social isolation and increase your sense of security in the long term.

It's often a big step to admit that you need outside help. Some people with social anxiety may even shy away from it - afraid of „exposing" themselves more in therapy or in front of friends. But it's worth taking the step and admitting it: You are not alone, and it is not a weakness to seek help. On the contrary, it often takes more courage to get help than to go through it alone.

Involve friends, family and your social environment

Our first subchapter is devoted to the most obvious, but sometimes the most difficult aspect: how to involve those close to you in the process. Many people find it challenging to talk openly about the fact that they have social anxiety disorder. They don't want to put a burden on those around them or fear that they won't be taken seriously. However, family and friends can provide real support if you are clear about your needs and fears.

Trust as a foundation
The most important foundation for successfully engaging others is trust - both in yourself („I can ask for help") and in those around you („They mean me no harm and are interested in my well-being").

Open conversation: It is helpful to have a calm conversation with a close family member or trusted friend. Explain what social anxiety means to you. It may be helpful to give specific examples - situations that make your heart race or make you feel panicky. This will help them understand what's going on with you.

Specific concerns: Rather than just expressing general complaints („I feel so anxious"), you can formulate what you want. For example: „When we meet in a larger group, it would be helpful if you would just ask me if everything is okay. Or if you don't ask me right away why I'm so quiet, just give me some time. Such clear questions are more concrete than vague wishes.

Share information: If you notice that people around you know little about social anxiety, you can provide them with easy-to-understand materials, such as a short educational video, pamphlet, or article. That way, they won't have to guess how to help you, but they will have a scientifically based insight.

Support in everyday life

It often helps if the people around you know and don't put pressure on you. Instead of asking: „Why are you so quiet?", they might offer to take a short break with you if they notice you getting anxious in the group.

Companionship: Some people find it helpful to have someone they trust by their side in difficult situations - for example, a close friend to accompany them to a doctor's appointment or to a meeting with new friends. This „safety net" can be gradually removed as you feel more stable.

Talk about your progress: Friends and family can motivate you by looking at your small progress together. Did they notice that you were less reserved than usual in a situation? How did that make you feel? This outside feedback can be a valuable mirror and give you more confidence.

Respect boundaries: At the same time, it is important for you and your loved ones to accept when you are not (yet) able to handle certain situations. You don't have to accept every invitation overnight. A loving „no" is better than forcing yourself to do something you are not ready for.

Difficulties in Dealing with Your Environment

People around you don't always respond with understanding. Sometimes family or friends will say: „Don't be like that" or „It's just shyness. This can be hurtful and reinforce your fears.

Patience: Try to be patient yourself. People often don't understand what social anxiety really means right away. They need time to think about it.

Set boundaries: If you find that certain people are torpedoing your process or repeatedly belittling you, you can reduce contact or set clear boundaries until they respect your path.

Alternative caregivers: If your family is not much help, good friends or other close confidants from your wider environment can step in - or you can seek professional support.

Professional help: therapy and counseling

While the social environment can provide emotional support, some challenges related to social anxiety are so complex that you may want to seek professional help. This may take the form of psychotherapy, coaching, or counseling, depending on the severity of your anxiety and your individual situation.

Types of psychotherapy
Cognitive Behavioral Therapy (CBT)
In the previous chapters, you learned about the principles of CBT: thought protocols, exposure, cognitive restructuring, and the development of positive beliefs. A trained therapist will guide you and give you feedback.

Depth Psychology Psychotherapy
Focuses on the unconscious causes of anxiety, often related to childhood experiences and relationship patterns. This can be helpful if you find that your social anxiety is closely related to old wounds.

Systemic therapy
This approach looks at your social environment as part of the system in which your anxiety arose. Systemic therapists examine the relationship dynamics that influence your behavior and how you can make positive changes.

Group therapy
Working in a group with other people with anxiety can be very helpful. You can learn new perspectives and practice social situations directly with people who have similar difficulties. It can often be the first place you feel successful.

Coaching and Counseling
Coaching is generally less deep psychological and more solution oriented. A coach helps you define specific goals (e.g., feel more confident in presentations) and develop action plans. Elements of CBT or systemic methods may be incorporated, but the focus is usually more on practical exercises and less on working through causes.

Counseling centers - e.g., universities, churches, social service agencies - often offer initial orientation sessions to determine if therapy is necessary or if coaching is sufficient. It is important to remember that seeking help is a sign of responsibility for yourself and not a sign of weakness.

How to Find a Good Therapist or Coach
Check qualifications: For therapists, look for a license in behavioral therapy or depth psychology, or at least a license under the German Heilpraktikergesetz (psychotherapy law). For coaches, recognized certifications such as ICF, DBVC, or systemic training may be a clue.

Personal chemistry: The level of rapport is critical. Do you feel understood and secure? Do you feel you can speak openly without being judged?

Define clear goals: In the first or second session, you and your counterpart should define what you want to work on. It's fine to adjust the goal later if your focus changes.

Cost: Psychotherapy with licensed therapists is usually covered by insurance (in many countries), whereas coaching is usually not. Find out in advance about costs and reimbursement options.

When professional help is most useful

There are situations in which professional help is strongly recommended:
- High levels of distress: You can barely cope with your daily life and avoid almost all social contact.
- Comorbid depression or other anxiety disorders: If you show signs of a depressive episode (e.g., listlessness, brooding, suicidal thoughts), it is important to seek professional help quickly.
- Complex trauma: If there are traumatic experiences in your past that contribute to your social anxiety, therapeutic support is almost essential.
- Long history of unsuccessful self-help strategies: If you have tried many things and still have not been able to stabilize yourself.

Online and self-help groups

In addition to the personal and professional environment, it can be very helpful to meet people who are in a similar situation. Many people report feeling alone, as if they are the only ones experiencing this type of anxiety. Support groups - offline or online - can be a great relief and can also provide many practical tips.

Benefits of support groups

Sense of community: You realize you are not alone. Others have similar thoughts and problems.

Exchange of experiences: You benefit from strategies that others have tried. Maybe someone has found a trick to be more relaxed in a group situation, and that idea could help you.

Motivation and accountability: The group can encourage you to stick to your goals, much like a team training together.

Feedback: In a trusting group, you can talk openly about your successes and failures and get honest feedback without being judged.

Offline groups

Many cities have local support groups specifically for social anxiety or anxiety disorders in general. You can find them through self-help agencies, notices in counseling centers, or search portals on the Internet. Groups usually meet weekly or bi-weekly to talk about personal challenges in a safe environment.

The hurdle of joining a new group with social anxiety can be daunting at first. But it can be a kind of exposure training: You put yourself in a safe space where others can relate to your own fears from their own experiences. If you feel uncomfortable, you can just listen at the first meeting and don't have to reveal anything about yourself right away.

Online communities and forums

If joining a real group is (still) too much for you, you can find like-minded people in online forums or social networks. You can sign up anonymously and chat at your own pace. The advantage of such communities is that you can access experiences and tips around the clock. However, you should be careful to maintain a respectful tone and guard against too much of a „negative spiral" - in some forums, members tend to reinforce each other's worries rather than promote constructive ideas for solutions.

There are also online support groups that meet via videoconference. This can be a good intermediate step if you don't have the confidence to show up in the analog world, but still want to be in contact with other sufferers.

Limitations of self-help

Support groups and online communities are valuable, but they are not a substitute for in-depth therapy if social anxiety is severe or if additional problems (such as depression or addiction) are present. Use these services as a supplement to professional help and your own work - not as a replacement if you feel you need more support.

The path to a greater sense of community

Humans are social creatures. Even if you feel introverted or insecure about interacting with others, a stronger sense of community can be an important resource for you. You might find a group that shares your interests (such as a choir, hiking group, or literature circle). Or you can volunteer by helping with an animal welfare organization or participating in a charity event.

All of these activities have one thing in common: they focus your attention away from your anxiety and toward a positive purpose. When you are doing something meaningful or participating in a community project, your self-doubt often fades into the background. You meet like-minded people and build relationships based on real collaboration, not just small talk.

Opportunities through community involvement

Personal growth: Every interaction can show you that you can work in a group without being constantly judged.

Positive sense of community: Completing a task together (e.g., organizing a summer party, running a fundraiser) makes you feel like part of a team. This builds self-esteem and social skills.

New perspectives: You will meet people who may come from different backgrounds. This broadens your horizons and sometimes puts your own problems into perspective.

Relief from pressure to perform: Many volunteer or cultural activities are not about efficiency, but about having fun together or achieving a common goal. You are often accepted more openly for who you are.

Beware of excessive demands

Of course, you must be careful not to throw yourself into too many things. Choose a level of community or commitment that you feel comfortable with. A very personal example might be meeting with a group once a week instead of taking on a board position or working in a facility with dozens of people every day. Make sure your step is big enough to challenge you, but not so big that you feel overwhelmed.

Community as a process

A sense of community doesn't happen overnight. It may take several meetings to build trust. Again, patience and an understanding that people thaw out at different rates in a group are needed. Keep at it, talk to individual group members if a large group is still too stressful for you, and give yourself time to grow into your role.

Summary and outlook

In this eighth chapter, the focus shifts from individual coping strategies to the social environment and professional support. The core message is that you don't have to do it all alone. It's perfectly fine, and often very beneficial, to involve people in your process - whether from your immediate environment, from a support group, or from your professional field.

Friends, family, and social circles can be supportive if they understand your social anxiety and are willing to respond to your needs.

Professional help through therapy or coaching is recommended if your anxiety is severe or if you have tried unsuccessfully to manage it on your own for a long time.

You can share experiences and motivate each other in online and support groups. You will see that others have similar experiences and can find additional inspiration.

A strong sense of community can develop when you get involved in volunteer or cultural projects. In this way, you create connections that give you a long-term sense of belonging.

In the next chapter, chapter nine, we look further ahead: „Looking Ahead: Growth and Prospects. Here you will learn how to align your knowledge and skills with the future. It's about finding meaning, personal development, and how to identify and seize new opportunities in your life. The goal is not just to free yourself from social anxiety, but to actively create the life you want.

In the meantime, take some time to consider: What kind of support is right for me? Do I want to get my family more involved first, or have I already thought about therapy? Is a support group appealing to me, or do I see myself in a small volunteer project in my favorite community? Every form of support has its value - the important thing is to take the first step in the direction that works best for you.

Remember, you are not alone. And you don't have to find your way out of social anxiety without help. On the contrary, being open to support is often the critical element that gives you the tailwind you need to achieve your goals and feel more confident in social situations.

Chapter 9: Looking ahead

The previous chapters have shown you that social anxiety does not have to be your fate. You have already learned many strategies for coping, from cognitive methods, mindfulness, and meditation to practical steps such as exposure training and targeted self-care. You may also have begun to build a support network, whether through your personal environment, professional support, or support groups.

But what happens next? How can you build on your newly acquired knowledge and initial successes in the long term, and at the same time develop new perspectives for your life? That is what this ninth chapter is all about: „Looking Ahead - Growth and Perspectives. Here we look at how you can turn your development to date into fertile ground for the rest of your life. You will discover that it is not just a matter of „overcoming fear," but of realizing your potential, which you may have underestimated for a long time.

Visions for your future

Why a positive vision of the future matters

Overcoming social anxiety is often about alleviating suffering and „not being afraid" of certain situations. This is a legitimate goal, but it may not be enough. For when the fear diminishes, a space opens up: What do you want instead? What opportunities do you want to seize, what adventures do you want to experience, what talents do you want to develop?

A vision of the future can help you overcome avoidance goals („I don't want to be so afraid anymore") and focus on attractors (magnetic desire images). The point is to develop a perspective that motivates and energizes you in your daily life, even when you are in danger of falling back into old patterns.

Characteristics of a Powerful Future Vision

Inspiring: A good vision makes you want to try something new, stimulates your imagination, and creates anticipation.

Realistic-optimistic: It can be ambitious, but not completely utopian, or it will quickly seem unattainable.

Personally meaningful: It is based on your values, dreams and interests, not the expectations of others.

Flexible: Your vision is not a dogma set in stone. It can evolve as you recognize that your path is changing.

Exercises for Developing Your Future Vision

Practice the ideal day: Imagine that you wake up tomorrow morning and your social anxieties play only a minor role in your life. What would your day be like? What would you do, who would you meet, what would you work on, how would you feel? Write it down or draw it.

Values Clarification: Take 10 to 15 minutes to write down values that are important to you-things like freedom, creativity, community, justice, love, adventure, security, or closeness to nature. Think about how you could live these values more in your daily life if you weren't constantly held back by fear.

Think about different areas of your life: Look at different areas - work, relationships, leisure, health, personal development. How would you like to grow in each area? How could you be open and courageous without overwhelming yourself?

Letter to your future self: Write a letter to yourself from the perspective of a point in the future (e.g., 6 or 12 months from now). Describe how you will be living, what you have learned, and what you are proud of. This letter can serve as a motivation and reminder later.

Exercises like this help you learn to shift your focus from simply reducing anxiety to positive visions. At the same time, you can become clearer about what concrete steps you need to take to achieve your goals and where your social anxiety is still getting in the way.

Finding meaning and personal development

Why Meaning Matters

People who suffer from social anxiety sometimes feel that they cannot participate in „normal" life. This can lead to deeper questions: „Why all this?" or „What is my place in society? Finding meaning means developing an inner compass that provides answers to these questions - a kind of guide to why it is worth facing the challenges rather than being limited by fear.

Motivation through purpose: When you have a strong „why," the „how" is easier. Your efforts to develop yourself no longer seem so exhausting or arbitrary, but have an emotional resonance.

Self-esteem: Meaning can provide a sense of significance-you feel that you are not just an „anxiety patient," but a person with skills and goals who wants to shape her life in a meaningful way.

Ways to find meaning

Self-reflection: Take regular time to reflect on questions such as „What makes me truly happy?", „What do I like to get up for in the morning?", „What experiences have been important to me?

Use sources of inspiration: Read books on personal development, philosophy, or biographies of people who inspire you. Talking with other people who live meaningful lives can also broaden your horizons.

Gain practical experience: Sometimes the only way to find out if something is meaningful is to try it, such as volunteering, doing a creative project, or traveling somewhere.

Be patient: Finding meaning is not a sprint. It's not a quick answer, but an ongoing examination of your values, goals, and interests.

Personal development as a way of life

Your future life after the intensive confrontation with social anxiety may become a life journey in which you not only reduce anxiety, but also realize yourself. This is also known as a „growth mindset": the belief that you can continually develop and acquire new skills. Experiencing how you can outgrow yourself and break old patterns can create a real sense of optimism: what else is possible?

This does not mean that you have to be constantly in action or live a perfect life. Rather, it's about staying open and willing to learn, and constantly challenging yourself. With each new experience that is not dominated by fear, your inner security grows, and you accumulate moments of growth that you can draw upon in the event of setbacks.

Discover new opportunities

Courage to seize opportunities
One of the most noticeable changes as your social anxiety decreases is that you can begin to recognize and take advantage of opportunities that previously caused you fear or panic. Maybe you used to think, „I'd love to do an internship abroad, but I don't dare, I don't know anyone there. Now you realize that although you still have respect for it, it no longer seems impossible.

The inner filter: Social anxiety can act as a filter that causes you to immediately reject potential opportunities as „too difficult" or „too risky. When you reduce the influence of this filter, you suddenly see opportunities that were previously hidden from you.

Yes, and... Principle: Instead of rejecting opportunities outright, you could try thinking „Yes, and..." more often. Example: „Yes, I'm still unsure, but I can prepare myself step by step.

Keep an open mind - even in the face of failure
Discovering new opportunities also means taking the risk that something might not work out the way you thought it would. A job you applied for may not be taken, a new acquaintance may turn out to be less than sympathetic, a creative project may fail. But that's part of growing. Failure does not mean that you are generally incapable or that you have fought your fears in vain.

On the contrary, you learn that life goes on when you take risks and possibly fail - and that you learn valuable lessons. The biggest difference is that you keep moving and evolving, rather than being afraid to take a chance. This creates a cycle of trial and error, success, failure, and new beginnings - all building blocks for a richer life.

Build a Compass of Possibility

Some people who have been blocked by social anxiety for a long time are initially unsure of how to identify or choose opportunities without overwhelming themselves. Here are some suggestions:

Your own values and visions (from chapters 9.1 and 9.2) can serve as a compass: Does a particular opportunity align with your values of freedom, creativity, or community?

Step-by-step approach: If something seems too big for you, an intermediate step can help. Would you like to join a theater group but are too intimidated? You might want to attend a rehearsal as an audience member or take a beginner's workshop first.

Control your fear response: Remember your methods from Chapter 5 (mindfulness, meditation, exposure) - you can apply them to new situations. Sometimes all you need to do is build up your inner security before you take the next step.

Gratitude and mindfulness in everyday life

Why Gratitude Changes Your Focus

If you have dealt with your social anxiety, you are familiar with the phenomenon of negative thought circles. These can easily cause you to overlook what is going well in your life or where you have made progress. Gratitude is a very effective way to focus on the positive - without denying the problems.

Psychologically proven: Numerous studies show that regular practice of gratitude exercises increases well-being and resilience.

Corrective: Gratitude corrects habitual perceptions by focusing not on shortcomings or failures, but on what is successful, helpful, and enriching.

Practical gratitude exercises

Daily gratitude journal: Take five minutes each evening to write down at least three things for which you are grateful that day. These can be small things (a friendly smile, a cup of good tea) or larger accomplishments.

Gratitude walk: Take a 10-15 minute walk and try to actively look for beautiful things - the light through the trees, the architecture of a house, the chirping of birds. Imagine saying „thank you" internally for each „find.

Thank-you letter: Write a short letter or email to a person who has supported you (e.g., a former teacher, therapist, friend) and thank them for what they have given you. This often results not only in joy for the recipient, but also a stronger sense of connection for you.

Gratitude meditation: Similar to mindfulness meditation, focus your attention on your body and breath. Then allow situations or people for whom you are grateful to appear before your inner eye and feel the resulting warmth or joy in your chest.

Mindfulness in everyday life

You can also apply the principles of mindfulness described in Chapter 5 to your everyday life. This means being mindful not only on the meditation cushion or during a quiet practice break, but also while doing the dishes, drinking coffee, waiting at traffic lights, or talking on the phone.

Mini Check-In: Once an hour, lift your head, briefly feel your body („How does my neck feel? How does my breath feel?"), and take a deep breath.

Take conscious breaks: When you are rushing from one task to another, take a few seconds each time to stop, relax your shoulders, and let your mind know: „I am now moving on to another activity.

One thing at a time: Multitasking often leads to stress and inattention. Instead, focus on one task until you complete it, or consciously interrupt it.

Small habits like these create a culture of mindfulness within you. You learn to perceive situations in the here and now and are much more likely to notice when your mood or anxiety arises. This gives you room to maneuver instead of being overwhelmed by an impulsive reaction.

Summary: Life beyond fear

This ninth chapter was about looking ahead and imagining what life could be like when social anxiety was no longer the focus. We came up with four aspects:

Visions of the future: It's not just about „no more anxiety," but about developing positive, inspiring goals that take you beyond your current limitations.

Meaning and personal development: A strong „why"-what you are committed to, what you live for-creates motivation and shifts the focus from avoidance to actively shaping your life.

Discover new possibilities: As fear subsides, opportunities that you previously blocked become visible. You learn to take small risks to unlock great potential.

Gratitude and mindfulness: These two attitudes help you to appreciate what you have achieved, to experience everyday life more consciously, and to always be in a constructive mood.

With every page you read in this book, you have created a piece of your path. Much of it is still theory, or perhaps already tested in small exercises. The next step is integration: integrating what you have learned into your daily life, experimenting, dealing with setbacks, and constantly opening up new possibilities.

What you can take away from this chapter

A vision is not just a nice mental game, it can become a real source of strength. Be clear about where you want to go, not just what you are running from.

Purpose and values are like an inner engine that propels you forward, even when fear tries to stop you.

Seizing new opportunities also means making mistakes and failing. But that is where true learning and growth lie.

Gratitude and mindfulness keep you mentally flexible. They protect you from endless brooding and always bring you back to the here and now, where real change happens.

A glimpse of your future path

Gradually, you will feel how what you have learned in this book affects more than just your social anxieties. Facing your fears and growing step by step into a more courageous approach to life can bring about a fundamental change. You regain your freedom of action, so to speak, and may discover completely new sides of yourself that were previously hidden under the cloak of fear.

Some people go down this path with the help of a therapist, others with the support of friends or like-minded people in a support group. Still others develop a personal spirituality or become politically, artistically, or socially active in an examination of their values. There is no one way to live after anxiety. The key is to be open to living by your own standards.

In the concluding Chapter 10, we will review the key findings and give you ideas for your next steps. Sometimes it is helpful to look back and reflect from a bird's eye view: What was important? What have I already implemented, and what's next?

Until then, I encourage you to stay curious. Social anxiety may have been „familiar" for a long time - uncomfortable, but familiar. Now you are entering new territory, making mistakes, celebrating successes, perhaps doubting again, and moving on. This process is human and part of any major change.

Dare to take a risk - whether it's a job interview, a new group of friends, or a spontaneous trip to a foreign city. Lovingly take your self-doubts by the hand and show them that you are still taking steps toward your goals. In time, doubts and fears will fade and confidence will grow in their place: „I can do more than I ever thought I could."

You have now completed Chapter Nine. You now have an idea of what is possible when you not only reduce your fear, but actively take control of your life. The next and final chapter will help you consolidate what you have learned, make concrete plans, and familiarize yourself with additional tools and resources. Look forward to the final part of this journey, which can only be the beginning of your new life of empowerment!

Chapter 10: Conclusion and outlook

Throughout this book, you have explored social anxiety, its causes, its many manifestations, and the many ways to deal with it. From understanding your own anxiety mechanisms to specific exposure training, cognitive restructuring, mindfulness exercises, targeted self-care, and building a supportive social network, you have been given a comprehensive overview of possible strategies. Now, at the end of this journey, it's time to take stock and look ahead to what's next.

Summary of the most important findings

Understanding instead of judging
Social anxiety is neither a personal failing nor a freak of nature. It is rooted in biological, familial, social, and personal experiences. Those who understand its mechanisms can deal with it more compassionately and clearly.

The Role of Negative Thoughts
Automatic and hypercritical thoughts have a huge impact on how you feel in social situations. Learning to recognize these thoughts, challenge them, and replace them with more realistic beliefs can reduce your anxiety.

Exposure: Dare to be brave
Whether you take small or large steps, exposing yourself to feared situations in controlled doses is still one of the most effective ways to reduce social anxiety in the long term. The gain in self-confidence is usually very noticeable.

Mindfulness, meditation, and relaxation
These methods help you to recognize and deal with emerging anxiety more calmly. They also promote the ability to accept your thoughts and feelings without being overwhelmed by them.

Self-care and self-confidence

Only those who are in touch with their own resources, interests, and values can manage anxiety in the long term. Positive beliefs, healthy routines, and a kind attitude toward yourself are the foundation for this.

Communication and social skills

People with social anxiety often shy away from conflict, networking or small talk. However, it is worthwhile to train these areas in small steps to gain more freedom in your personal and professional life.

Find support

You don't have to do it alone. Family, friends, support groups, or professional help from therapists and coaches are valuable resources. Sharing your experiences with others can be very reassuring and encouraging.

Growth and perspective

When social anxiety no longer dominates your life, there is room for meaningful vision and personal growth. Gratitude and mindfulness in daily life help you recognize progress and take advantage of new opportunities.

What happens next: your next steps

Check your personal toolbox
You may have already discovered some exercises or strategies in the chapters that particularly appeal to you. Write down what you would like to practise regularly (e.g. breathing exercises, cognitive restructuring, exposure in small doses). Think about the times of day or week when you can realistically use these tools.

Design your own support network
Take a look at where you are now: do you already have people around you who understand and support you? Or would you like to join a self-help group or start therapy? Don't be afraid to take the next step in this direction.

Define and share goals
Setting realistic goals helps you not to overwhelm yourself. Start with small goals, e.g: „Attend a group meeting once a week and speak up at least once". When you realize that you can do it, you can set your goal higher.

Document your progress
A small notebook or diary will help you to record your progress and setbacks. This creates a tangible record of your development over time. If in doubt, you can read up on the hurdles you have already overcome.

Plan for setbacks

Accept that not every day will be perfect. There may be phases in which anxiety returns more strongly. Don't see this as a failure, but as a natural part of the change process. Use the techniques you have learned and seek additional support if necessary.

Tools and outlook

With this book, you have a guide that will take you through a wide range of topics, from the origins of social anxiety to practical exercises and a positive vision of the future. Ultimately, what matters is what you take away for your everyday life.

Here are some final tips to help you manage your social anxiety and develop your skills:

Regular self-reflection
Continue to think about where you are. What has changed? Which exercises have become part of your daily routine, and which have been neglected? Do you want to start them again or try something new?

Encouragement from role models
There may be people in your life or famous people who have struggled with anxiety and now seem very confident. Talk to them or read their stories. You may find encouragement and concrete suggestions.

Be open to change
Even if you have achieved a lot, a certain amount of flexibility is helpful. New life transitions (job change, relocation, new relationships) bring new challenges - and opportunities to learn and grow.

Celebrate your successes
Don't forget to be proud of yourself. Every situation you have mastered, every new conversation you have had, every time you have said „yes" to life when fear tried to whisper „no" - all are valuable and should remind you of how far you have come.

Concluding words

Social anxiety can severely limit your life, but it doesn't have to. By understanding it, dealing with it, activating your inner resources, and creating a supportive environment, you can change your perspective step by step. The journey is not always easy, but every change in your thoughts and actions, no matter how small, has the potential to open new, unexpected doors.

The end of this book is not the beginning of a rigid „after" for you, but an ongoing process. You now have the tools to reduce social anxiety and live a more open and confident life. Feel free to revisit each chapter if you feel you're stuck. Take what you need and implement it step by step at your own pace.

From now on, it's up to you: Where do you want to go? What relationships do you want to cultivate, what goals do you want to pursue, how do you want to deal with yourself? May the strategies you learn and the deepened understanding of yourself help you move forward - and create a life that fulfills you and is right for you.

You are not at the mercy of your path. You can actively shape it. This is perhaps the most important insight you can take away from this book. I wish you courage, patience, compassion for yourself, and many small and large successes to show you the way: You are more than your fear.

Did you like the book? Please rate it on Amazon, it would be a great help to me! Thank you very much.

If you have any questions or concerns, you can reach me at any time at: impressum.berger@proton.me.

Printed in Great Britain
by Amazon